Thoughts on Francis of Assisi

AMERICAN UNIVERSITY STUDIES

SERIES VII
THEOLOGY AND RELIGION

Vol. 339

PETER LANG
New York · Washington, D.C./Baltimore · Bern
Frankfurt am Main · Berlin · Brussels · Vienna · Oxford

LATIFAH TRONCELLITI

Thoughts on Francis of Assisi

PETER LANG
New York · Washington, D.C./Baltimore · Bern
Frankfurt am Main · Berlin · Brussels · Vienna · Oxford

Library of Congress Cataloging-in-Publication Data

Troncelliti, Latifah.
Thoughts on Francis Of Assisi / Latifah Troncelliti.
pages cm. — (American university studies. VII, Theology and religion; v. 339)
Includes bibliographical references and index.
1. Franciscans—Rules. 2. Franciscans—History.
3. Francis, of Assisi, Saint, 1182–1226. I. Title.
BX3604.Z5T76   271'.3—dc23   2013029604
ISBN 978-1-4331-2443-3 (hardcover)
ISBN 978-1-4539-1205-8 (e-book)
ISSN 0740-0446

Bibliographic information published by **Die Deutsche Nationalbibliothek.**
Die Deutsche Nationalbibliothek lists this publication in the "Deutsche
Nationalbibliografie"; detailed bibliographic data is available
on the Internet at http://dnb.d-nb.de/.

The paper in this book meets the guidelines for permanence and durability
of the Committee on Production Guidelines for Book Longevity
of the Council of Library Resources.

© 2013 Peter Lang Publishing, Inc., New York
29 Broadway, 18th floor, New York, NY 10006
www.peterlang.com

All rights reserved.
Reprint or reproduction, even partially, in all forms such as microfilm,
xerography, microfiche, microcard, and offset strictly prohibited.

Printed in Germany

Contents

Introduction 1

1 The Assisi Compilation: On Broken Mirrors 5

2 The Medieval Canonization Process:
  Reality and Politics. *Vox Populi, Vox Dei?* 17

3 Saints and Demons in Medieval Space. 33

4 *Sacrum Commercium* 51

5 Franciscan Women 59

6 The Unbearable Lightness of Francis' *Forma Vitae* 73

Bibliography 115

Index 121

Introduction

This is a collection of essays written during a three-year research on Church history at the Institute of Franciscan Studies at St. Bonaventure University. Each essay describes a different aspect of Franciscan history since the time of Francis of Assisi (1182-1226), founder of the Franciscan Order. All essays, however, have a common theme: the Franciscan Order's makeover devised by the Catholic Church after Francis' death. The Franciscan Order was never what Francis had created. Francis had understood the needs of his time and with his brothers had organized a social structure to counteract the corruption of contemporary society. His rule for the *Fratres Minores,* the original Franciscan Order, was meant to establish peace and equality among people who worked together in a community, yet each using his own particular talent: an ideal that had a short life. At Francis' death Pope Gregory IX took the opportunity to use Francis' popularity in order to satisfy his political ambition. Despite the protest of Francis' closest brothers and sisters, the ones who had shared the true experience of the order during his life, the Pope changed Francis' *forma vitae* into something more palatable and useful to the Church. Most of the new friars, in fact, preferred a less rigorous rule and were in favor of an easier lifestyle under the Church's protection. The Franciscan Order became a tool for the Church to reassert control on every issue and in every situation regarding spirituality, religious dogmas, the position of women in society and material possessions. Many of these issues had never been on Francis' agenda. While making of

Francis a famous saint with a spectacular canonization, at the same time the Church ignored Francis' original and revolutionary concept often deeply opposed to the Church's politics.

The ambiguity of the Church's position is still evident in modern scholarship. It reflects the confusion surrounding historical happenings pertinent to Francis' life and deeds. It is no secret that after Francis'death the Church destroyed most documents that could shed light on Francis' real experience. The Church has made of Francis a pious saint, an imaginary creature that had submitted to Catholic doctrine, thus useful to its political power. This attitude did not change through the centuries. By now the real Francis is totally unknown and modern scholars are still debating the Franciscan Question. Who was Francis?

The essays express personal thoughts on Francis and on the Franciscan Order past and present, which not necessarily reflect an orthodox view. I dedicate these essays to Dr. Michael Cusato OFM, whose knowledge and open-mindedness brightened my days throughout my study. My deepest thanks also to all the professors at the Franciscan Institute who helped me in my work: I am grateful for their dedication, patience and willingness to listen to my questions and comments. Many thanks to Dr. Frank Bianco, who helped editing the manuscript.

Here is a brief summary that defines the subject of each essay. The first essay deals with the lack of information about Francis' real story. In the *Assisi Compilation*, one of the most famous writings in Franciscan production, it is evident that historians according to their own religious tendency freely interpreted the ambiguity of Franciscan hagiography. The *Assisi Compilation* shows clearly the impossibility of arriving to a sure understanding of Francis' life. His deeds are surrounded by a deep obscurity, which has been even more exacerbated by the Church's determination to use Francis' great popularity to manipulate his intentions in favor of its struggle for material power.

The second essay is dedicated to the procedure of canonization. The canonization appears to be an anomaly when compared to other great religious systems. By scratching just so slightly the surface of this historical phenomenon it is possible to recognize its tremendous political benefit for the papacy. The exploitation by the Catholic Church of the popularity of each canonized saint becomes clear particularly when we examine the case of the most famous Franciscsan saints such as Saint Francis of Assisi and Saint Anthony of Padua. This essay proposes to discover the real purpose under the magic scenario of the canonization process.

The third essay puts in perspective the medieval socio-economic structure that underlies the development of religious institutions. In this essay we examine in particular women's place in a society that precludes them from the possibility of choosing freely their destiny. The Franciscan communities mushrooming in Italy and in the whole of Europe are not different. They follow the mold established by the Roman Church, fearful of the feminine potential for destabilizing and threatening a misogynist society. Already during Francis' lifetime, and increasingly afterward, Franciscan women were forced to live in reclusion. From this treatment there were psychological and emotional consequences that resulted in the aberrant phenomenon of excessive ascetic practices that were often confused with spirituality. Francis certainly did not contemplate this development in the life of Franciscan women in his *forma vitae*. A famous and glamorous case has been that of Margherita da Cortona, who is still to this day venerated as a saint.

The fourth essay attempts to find the real Francis, mission impossible perhaps, but still worth the effort. Only one among many manuscripts of Franciscan tradition, the *Sacrum Commercium,* seems to tell us the truth as many scholars believe. It is a grand scenario in which Lady Poverty, Francis' love, plays the major role. The tale does not give historical details, but it testifies to the brothers' unhappiness at the Roman Church's betrayal of Francis' spirit. We understand that perhaps already during the last years of Francis' life there was a wide sense of discontent among the older friars who had known and experienced the *forma vitae* by living it together with Francis. They wanted to maintain Francis' Early Rule as a central part of their daily life. The Church in the person of the Pope effected a major change that transformed the Franciscan community into a pale shadow of the original order.

The fifth essay examines the life of Franciscan women and the development of their organization from a community of laywomen, later called beguines, to a life in a monastery. After Francis' death the communal spirit of the brotherhood, at first shared equally by men and women, soon disappeared. The Church took complete control of the women's lives and did not allow lay communities. Franciscan women, as all other religious women, were forbidden to have an active life outside a convent. The story of the Monastery of Santa Lucia in Foligno, however, is an example of how women, even constrained by the Church's rules to live in an enclosed space, were capable of exercising their intellectual and literary talents that transformed their community in a *scriptorium* brimming with creative activity.

The intention of the last essay is to explore the delicate balance between work and poverty as conceived by Francis and his brothers in the Early Rule. They declared their vision for a new system of relationships between their community and the society at large. The social structure that Francis created could have satisfied human needs at all levels of existence, from the most basic necessity for food and shelter, and the emotional need of support from their brothers and sisters, to the creative energy with which each of them could contribute to the building of a sustainable community. The secret was work: working together in accord with each personal talent would have given the impulse for a vital, peaceful life respectful of individual ability. Through the texts available to us it appears that there has been a gradual deformation of Francis' original intent. After a close look to the Early Rule and its reformulation into the Later Rule, the writings of three eminent Franciscan personalities, Hugh of Digne, Peter of John Olivi and Angelo Clareno are important for understanding to what extent their attempt to reach back to Francis' first *propositum vitae* was fraught by misinterpretation. The question is: why and how did it happen that the intellectual sophistication of great scholars could not perceive the reality and simplicity of Francis' *forma vitae*? Many questions remain unanswered, but it can be said that Francis was real, although his message of peace and beauty was a brief happening lived by few exceptional beings and never to be repeated.

CHAPTER ONE

THE ASSISI COMPILATION

ON BROKEN MIRRORS

In his comedy *Così è se vi pare* (*Right you are if you think so, 1917*) the Italian writer Luigi Pirandello adequately expressed the feeling of dismay for the infinite reflections of a newly discovered kaleidoscopic reality.[1] Moreover, so uncomfortable and upset was the public at the first representation of another one of Pirandello's famous comedies, *Sei personaggi in cerca di autore* (*Six characters in search of an author, 1921*), that the author had to run out of the theatre Valle in Rome followed by an angry crowd of enraged spectators. A second representation was not possible until later when a more sensitive audience, in Milan, did not recoil from the perception of possible multiple selves and from contradictory notions about the very concept of identity. It was about at the same time in Italy that the writer Italo Svevo confronted the complexity of consciousness in his novel *La coscienza di Zeno* (*Zeno's conscience, 1923*).[2] The end of the nineteenth century and the beginning of the twentieth century was a time for hard questions that opened up the gate of individual perception. We cannot forget that in 1913 Einstein published his theory of relativity while Marcel Proust (1871- 1922), traveling within his conscience, wrote *À la recherche du temps perdu* (*In Search of Lost Time*). Consciousness took a leap

---

1   Luigi Pirandello (1867-1936) is an Italian playwrite who brought a new understanding to the concept of identity. *Così è (se vi pare)* (*Right you are if you think so*) in 1925 is one of his most popular comedies, dealing with the multiple perception of identity.

2   Italo Svevo (1861-1928) is an Italian writer completely ignored by critics and readers at the time of publication of his main work in 1923, *La coscienza di Zeno*.

toward a more expanded awareness of itself and its surroundings. Most questions dealt with the discovery of new realities hidden behind a longstanding belief system; many remained without answers.

In religious studies Paul Sabatier (1858-1928) broke centuries of peaceful silence on our Italian favored saint, Francis of Assisi, introducing doubts and criticism on his identity. For a longtime the image of our Italian patron saint had appeared sweet and smiling gently to all creatures until Sabatier began hunting for manuscripts that could resolve his doubts. He actually found them and the *Franciscan Question* came into existence. The quest for a new, true Francis, the unknown Francis hidden behind his century-old identity, began in earnest and kept growing with Sabatier's painstaking work of reconstruction soon imitated by many others. The public exposed to Pirandello's theatrical lucubration or Svevo's readers led through the meander of Zeno's consciousness were just as confused and upset as a reader can be when confronted by the *Franciscan Question*.

Of course, the fact that Sabatier was a protestant Frenchman made the reaction among Catholic scholars particularly virulent, because Francis is certainly the Catholic Italian saint par excellence. A frenetic activity ensued in which manuscripts were edited and reedited. Entire texts were arbitrarily moved from one manuscript to another one. Old material was reworked in new editions with new attractive titles, thus transformed in seemingly new discoveries as more appealing intellectual adventures ready made to the scholars' delight. Among the numerous works produced by all the great scholars who have been and are protagonists of the *Franciscan Question* the most puzzling is the *Assisi Compilation*, so called because it is precisely a compilation of different texts that have little to do with each other besides finding themselves gathered in the same manuscript. According to the introduction in *Francis of Assisi, Early Documents*[3] the *Assisi Compilation* is a text produced after Minister General Crescentius' request in 1244 that called for a gathering of stories about Francis and his early brotherhood. The *Assisi Compilation* was found in the manuscript 1046 of the *Biblioteca Augusta* of Perugia and was first published in 1922 by Ferdinand Delorme; it was originally in the library of the *Sacro Convento* of Assisi, because it appears in an inventory of 1381. The manuscript includes a papal decree dated 1310 by Clement V, thus most scholars agree that it must have been written after that date and give as a possibility the year 1311 when Ubertino da Casale mentioned its existence.[4] Scholars did not discover who the author was, but, if we consider the difference in content and style throughout the manuscript, most likely the compilation is the product of many authors who wrote at different times. It is possible that some material was copied from

---
3   *Francis of Assisi, Early Documents II*, 114-116.
4   Ibid., 113.

the famous Leo's scroll, as Ubertino da Casale suggested. A cause of great confusion is the variety of different titles used to describe the content of Ms 1046. In the introduction to the *Assisi Compilation* we find a mind-boggling array of titles[5] referring to various interpretations of the same manuscript.

After a first acknowledgment in 1922, Delorme isolated in the Ms 1046 the material in *Celano's Second Life of Francis* and published the rest in 1926 as *Legenda Perusina or Legenda di Perugia*. In 1970 Rosalind Brook decided to do something different from what Delorme had done. She published at Oxford her book *Scripta Leo-Angelo-Rufino* in which she republished Delorme's work and rearranged it in a new shape as a *Legenda* with the title *The Three Companions*. She attached to her work the *Letter of Greccio*. In this case the reworking of Delorme's *Legenda* was a mistake that created confusion among scholars: *The Three Companions* was precisely what Leo, Angelo and Rufino, the writers of the *Letter of Greccio* to Minister General Crescentius da Iesi, denied to have written. They went all the way to define their work not as a *Legenda*, but as an anthology (*florilegium*) of different stories they had collected through the years. The stories did not have relation between them and were not in chronological order. Brook did not help to clarify Franciscan history, but finally Marino Bigaroni had the best idea: he called the texts precisely what they were, that is, a collection of writings, a *Compilation*, and he reclaimed the work for Assisi, because the manuscript appeared first in Assisi in the library of the *Sacro Convento* as it resulted from the convent's inventory of 1381. The *Assisi Compilation* was better defined by Bigaroni's intervention in 1975.

Something else happened to make things more interesting. In his *Nos qui cum eo fuimus, Contributo alla questione francescana* (1980), Raoul Manselli followed the pattern Delorme had indicated. He worked on the *Legenda Perusina* studying in particular the expression *Nos qui cum eo fuimus* (*We who were with him*), often found in the manuscript. He advanced the proposition that the formula *Nos qui cum eo fuimus*, repeated in many texts, could only mean that the writing was the work of Francis' early companions, the ones who witnessed with their presence Francis' life and deeds. In his conclusive considerations Manselli strove to find consistency and argued that *Nos qui cum eo fuimus* was always used with a specific intent and was a necessary corollary to the particular situation the writer described. For example, referring to *Legenda Perusina* 11, Manselli arguably stated:

> Qui la formula risponde alla necessità di una testimonianza oculare di quanto essi raccontano e cioè che si recava a pregare quando veniva maltrattato e che ritornando non voleva più sentirne parlare in un' umiltà perfetta [...] Qui l'essere stati con Francesco

---
5   Ibid., 113.

segue a garantire la veridicità di averlo visto e di aver visto qualcosa che faceva soffrire il Santo e non faceva onore ai suoi confratelli.[6]

It is hard to prove the necessity of an eyewitness in this particular story more than it would be necessary in all other narrations where the formula is not found: all the texts are equally important to define Francis' individuality. The impression is that Manselli is riding on his profound admiration for Francis and constructing an artificial imagery to justify it. His interpretation of texts is literal and colored by sentimental tones; whenever he finds the *Nos qui cum eo fuimus* he believes every single word without criticism. In his interpretation he projects the sweet and heroic image of the classic Francis of hagiographic literature. Firmly convinced of his hypothesis, Manselli could not accept the point of view that the formula *Nos qui cum eo fuimus* is nothing else but a rhetorical tool, a *topos* already used with the same intent, for example, in the *Gospel of Saint John XIX / 35, XXI / 24* and also, in the *Historia Lausiaca* in Migne, *LXXIII, 1160, 1156*.[7] He criticized Nino Tamassia, professor of law at the University of Padua, who wrote a sharp and believable critical interpretation of Franciscan writings. Tamassia is not a well-known scholar but he makes interpretative suggestions that would deserve further study. For sure he caught this reader's attention.

What do we make of the *Assisi Compilation*? Historically we cannot establish the exact time when the texts were written, because they are so different in style and content. They might represent the image of Francis as it evolved from his lifetime through 1244-1260. But nothing is sure. The *Assisi Compilation* is a broken mirror: from each shiny piece a different image of Francis comes forth. In this collection of stories-images we find the representations, fantasies, dreams and desires that people constructed through time to satisfy their individual needs and aspirations. Every image reflected in each piece of the broken mirror may be true or false at the same time. *Così è se vi pare*, Pirandello would say: Francis is whatever you want him to be. In any case we do not have any proof of his real life and deeds except for the scattered reflections of a broken mirror. It comes to mind how the image of a mirror, *speculum*, was often used in the Middle Ages as a symbol of truth. The *Speculum Perfectionis, A Mirror of Perfection*, was the first work of Franciscan literature published by Sabatier in 1898. This work was written possibly at

---

6 Raoul Manselli, *Nos qui cum eo fuimus, Contributo alla questione francescana.* (Roma: Istituto Storico dei Cappuccini, 1980), 239. Trans.: "Here the formula demonstrates the necessity of an eyewitness for what they are narrating, that is, he went to pray when friars mistreated him and coming back he did not want to talk about it, in perfect humility […] Here the fact of having been with Francis insures the truth of having seen him and also of having seen something that caused suffering to the Saint and shame to his brothers."

7 Nino Tamassia, *San Francesco d'Assisi e la sua leggenda.* (Padova, Verona: Fratelli Drucker, 1906), 135, n2.

about the same time as the *Assisi Compilation* and in fact it shows the same signs of change in the brothers' mentality found in many passages of the *Assisi Compilation*. The *Speculum Perfectionis*, however, has the goal of reminding the brothers of *the Rule, Profession, Life and True Calling of a Lesser Brother,* thus it has a consistency totally lacking in the disconnected fragments of the *Assisi Compilation*. Since Sabatier's first critical approach the effort to make sense out of a diverse and confusing material has been the main occupation of Franciscan scholars and after all it must be recognized that their work resulted in interesting discoveries. A feeling of great excitement was unavoidable while so many learned scholars cut, pasted and sifted through the texts and turned them upside down in search of the true Francis.

There was a strong need to find a logical lead that could give a realistic image of Francis. Manselli attempted a unified vision of Francis under the umbrella of the *Nos qui cum eo fuimus* in the *Legenda Perusina*. His interpretation strongly influenced Franciscan scholars. Jacques Dalarun, however, even admiring Manselli for his research, has doubts on Manselli's proposal that the formula *Nos qui cum eo fuimus* could introduce the real facts straight from Francis' life. He argued: "[...] the question remains whether they wanted, in good faith, to emphasize passages that agreed with their idea and memory of the saint. [...]"[8] We will never know. Dalarun is also more upfront than other scholars because, while diplomatically stating his admiration for everybody else, he does not hesitate to give a realistic look to the actual situation. Concerning the *Legenda di Perugia* he stated right away: "Let us try to be clear about what the *Legend of Perugia* is. It is an artificial construct. Or rather, it is a working hypothesis."[9] Dalarun proceeded to explain the complex history behind Ms 1046 and recognized at the end that what he had done "is a questionable summary, is the minimum we need to know about the *Assisi Compilation* and the *Legend of Perugia*."[10] And again he commented: "For once, study of the earlier sources is no help in clarifying the text of the legend [...]."[11]

There is a positive side: while Francis seems lost forever or lives only in people's dreams, the most interesting aspect of the *Assisi Compilation* is the evolution of how Francis was imagined and how his image was construed at the service of his followers. It does help to understand the mentality of the time and how political power and social events influenced the historical environment to which people had to adjust and react. Let us see then some of the con-

---

8   Jacques Dalarun, *The Misadventure of Francis of Assisi*. (St. Bonaventure, NY: Franciscan Institute, 2002), 38.
9   Ibid., 204.
10 Ibid., 205.
11 Ibid., 206.

traditions in the texts that might show the evolution of the Franciscan Order from Francis' time to the fourteenth century.

The text AC 17 reflects the tension among the brothers that already existed during Francis' life and slowly reached a breaking point. Francis was losing control over the brotherhood particularly concerning the acceptance of the *Rule*, now at the center of many disputes that kept growing after his death in 1226. Francis was shown reacting passionately against the current event, but is it really Francis' or his brothers' reaction projected from a future writer into Francis' image? In the story Francis does not appear sweet and humble, his usual characteristic aspects that place him above worldly preoccupation. He reacts in human terms, finally human, and the reader welcomes his humanity. To the rude assertion of Elias ("make it for yourself and not for them") who reports his brothers' anxiety for the possible extreme hardship of a new rule, Francis responds addressing himself to Christ and Christ answers through him with a passion never expressed before. That is Francis' passion: "[…] I want the Rule to be observed in this way: to the letter, to the letter, to the letter, and without a gloss, without a gloss, without a gloss […]."[12] The repetitions are extraordinarily expressive of Francis' will and of his disappointment for his brothers' lack of faith. We find the same tone of anger and also the feeling of being cornered in an inacceptable role in the following text, AC 18. This time Francis deals with Cardinal Hugolino who is trying to convince him to accept one of the already existing Rules such as the Rule of Benedict, of Augustine or Bernard. One small detail in the story suggests that in this short paragraph, in a small fragment of the broken mirror, we are perhaps seeing reflected the real Francis we love. We feel the sweetness and greatness of Francis' gesture when he takes the cardinal by the hand. Francis is now the father figure who patiently explains the truth to his young son:

> Then blessed Francis, on hearing the cardinal's advice, *took him by the hand* (my emphasis) and led him to the brothers assembled in chapters and spoke to the brothers in this way: "My brothers, my brothers […] The Lord told me what he wanted: He wanted me to be a new fool in the world. God did not wish to lead us by any way other than his knowledge, but God will confound you by your knowledge and wisdom. […] Through them He will punish you, and you will return to your state, to your blame, like it or not." The cardinal was shocked and said nothing and all the brothers were afraid.[13]

In this fragment Francis is present in all his human nature, at the same time exalted and inspired by his spiritual experience. The text well represents a credible and powerful personality, sweet but also firm in his belief in di-

---

12 *Early Documents II*, 132.

13 Ibid., 132-133.

vine inspiration. Well, it is true that his projection into a future in which his brothers would have repented never was to come true. Even saints have their blind spots. In any case the two stories sound plausible, but with caution: it is possible that they were real memories of Francis' early companions who witnessed Francis' reaction. It is also possible, however, that in the later years when it became evident that the brotherhood was changing direction from the original intent the companions who wanted to be faithful to Francis expressed their own disappointment projected into Francis' behavior.

Contradictions also exist in the description of Francis' lifestyle, for example, concerning food or clothing. As Dalarun notes, in many episodes Francis was very flexible about any restriction. He respected individual freedom in regard of particular circumstances that might require different personal decisions. Francis recommended his brothers not to be too harsh on their bodies; he was basically against harsh penances or asceticism. The *Assisi Compilation*, however, often stated that he was extremely severe to his body that suddenly he considered an enemy and treated as such. While the original approach to food was very relaxed and practically followed the advice given in *Luke 10.8* ("Let us eat…what has been placed before us."[14]), in the *Assisi Compilation* there are fragments in which the contrary occurs. For example in AC 80, Francis ordered Peter Cattani "to lead him naked with a rope tied around his neck in front of people…." That is because he felt he had indulged in delicacies while he was seriously ill and wanted to punish his body. It is curious also that he contradicted himself on the principle of obedience to a superior. In fact by resigning to his office in the Order he had committed himself to obey Peter Cattani, who was at the time acting as Minister General, and his guardian. In this text he is shown as taking back control, commanding Peter "to obey and not contradict whatever he wanted to say or do to himself." Indeed it is quite odd for Francis to make such a request. Is it spiritual pride that took over his humility and total surrender? Are these several episodes, in which Francis expressed strong distaste for his body and a masochistic desire to punish it, emblematic of a later development? They might reflect devolution from the original spirit and a return to the monastic ascetic lifestyle that many Franciscan brothers and sisters practiced in monasteries in the fourteenth-fifteenth centuries, when Francis' spirit had already disappeared within the Catholic Church. Francis then became a champion in the heroic negation of bodily needs, something unknown to the joyous celebration of life in the first Franciscan *fraternitas*.

The general attitude toward his companions and other people in the stories is also puzzling, because Francis is represented as oscillating between a permissive approach, desiring to help with understanding and great patience, and a harsh attitude that showed exasperation and lack of forgiveness. An ex-

---
14 Dalarun, 207.

ample of the first approach is a beautiful episode that Dalarun mentioned.[15] In AC115 Francis is able to turn around a precarious situation with some robbers who used to assault passersby near the hermitage in Borgo San Sepolcro. With patience and humility Francis was able to convert them by simply giving them what they needed and thus changed their mind-set: "Some entered religion, others embraced penance promising in the hands of the brothers no longer to commit these evil deeds but to live by the work of their hands."[16] The episode brings us back to the classic, more popular, Francis, who took Hugolino by the hand to show him the truth. Right after, though, in AC 116 Francis suddenly became hard and unforgiving. His understanding of others disappeared: Francis revealed that a brother who was considered a saint was an impostor and mercilessly put him to test. It is a gruesome story because at the end the brother was forced to leave the community and after few days he died alone. In another similar story, AC70, Francis refused to let in the order the young son of a nobleman from Lucca. Francis' words to the young nobleman make no sense unless Francis is going through a spiritual crisis perhaps thinking of his own dissolute youth, who knows? It seems strange that Francis' brothers find the episode uplifting: "The brothers and others, who were there, marveled, magnified, and praised God in his Saint."[17] As Dalarun pointed out there are many examples of this type of inconsistency in the *Assisi Compilation*, so much that he wrote: "The contrast between the two attitudes is such that I can only call certain passages in the *Legend of Perugia* distorted."[18] Yes, distorted by Francis' later followers who transformed the once true brotherhood, *fraternitas*, in a rigid system without any brotherly relationship. Or is it possible that the imagination we have had for centuries of a Francis full of love, peaceful and understanding to all, could have been precisely that, an imagination? According to Dalarun the *Legend of Perugia* is an artificial construct. For what we know Francis as well could have been a historical artificial construct that compensated a human need for love and peace during a horrifying time of wars, inquisition and pestilence: a triumph of human imagination.

The incongruence in Francis' images in the *Assisi Compilation* is so staggering that an entire book could be written to cover all of them. Their subtlety and significance are important for detecting the dramatic change undergone in Franciscan history from Francis' requests stated in his *Rule* to the official Franciscan Order created, not by Francis, but by Hugolino, Pope Gregory IX. Certainly, at least according to our imagined lovable Francis, the Order ceased to be what Francis would have wanted: a *fraternitas*.

---

15 Dalarun, 210.

16 *Early Documents*, 222.

17 Ibid., 173.

18 Dalarun, 211.

One more contrasting aspect deserves to be mentioned because it touches on a characteristic quality of Francis: his appreciation, strong connection and respect for the natural world. His *Cantico delle Creature* is symbolic of his love for all creatures. We find in the *Assisi Compilation* several stories that eloquently illustrate this admirable quality. In AC 14, a flock of larks sings above the hut where he is dying. The writer explains that Francis loved all birds but especially loved his sister lark: "Our Sister Lark has a capuche like religious, and is a humble bird, who gladly goes along the road looking for some grain. Even if she finds it in the animal's manure, she pecks out and eats it...."[19] So he loved the larks more than other birds for their resemblance to the brothers. Even though it does not sound like a great motivation for favoring the larks it is at least about love. About love is also a tender image of Francis whom Sister Cricket consoled at the *Portiuncula* in AC 110, but love changed into fear and aversion when we read, in AC 83, of mice that bothered Francis day and night "so much so that his companions, and he himself, considered it a temptation of the devil, which it was."[20] At the same time that Francis considered mice a diabolic manifestation he was writing his famous *Cantico delle creature* that celebrated all creatures. We have here a drastic change in attitude toward animals; it is incongruent that at the same time Francis showed impatience against mice he was composing a glorious lyric honoring all of God's creatures. Is it possible that a late, not very perceptive writer could distort the content creating inconsistency in the story? We cannot doubt the existence of the *Cantico*. This enchanting poem does exist as the first example of Italian literature, but being in the mood for questioning can we be absolutely sure that Francis wrote it? Or perhaps Brother Pacifico *the King of Verses* wrote it? [21] Which Francis do we choose? Francis of the larks and crickets or Francis of mice? Dalarun comments: "His conviction and that of the brothers was that the infestation of mice was the work of the devil. So then, while crickets and larks are at once such lovable creatures, why should mice be creatures of the devil? Why should contact with them be more distressing than contact with lepers or with a red-hot iron?"[22] In fact, we have to acknowledge in many passages an increasing appearance of demons or diabolic entities that tempted or wanted to harm Francis; they even hid inside his pillow and did not let him sleep. The harmonious balance of our Francis' life, the imagined spontaneity of his spiritual experience is lost among a new array of concerns dealing with the negative forces of creation. A narrow interpretation of spirituality based upon a strict dualism

---

19 *Early Documents* II, 129-130.

20 Ibid., 185. The same passages are commented on by Dalarun, 212.

21 *Early Documents, the Prophet.* 59, 304: "[...] Brother Pacific, who in the world had been known as *King of Verses*, a noble and courtly master of singers."

22 Dalarun, 212.

was progressively more frequent as time went by after Francis' existence: bad versus good, body versus soul and the demonic and angelic forces typical of medieval religious beliefs became increasingly more intense. They must instill fear and submission in the Church's acolytes in order to control their behavior. From the early thirteenth to fourteenth century a lot has changed and the later writers or copyists of the *Assisi Compilation* expressed their own faith mixed up with old Franciscan stories. The images that emerge from the broken mirror suggest a growing rigidity in religious structure and less space for individual spiritual freedom. So far there are more and more questions and all without plausible answers. Scholars would need another unexpected manuscript to pop up from some unknown library, ideally the famous Leo's scroll. What a joy that would be.

The reader is not at ease. Even within the limit of available material, not absolutely everything has been truly explored about Francis. Franciscan studies focus on the Franciscan brotherhood with a magnifying lens often excluding other important factors active in concomitance with Francis' experiment. Scholars, particularly among Catholics, often forget to look at the surrounding environment, at the brothers' interaction with other people of different background in the wide world outside the Church. The Catholic Church was not the sole reality in Francis' time. There were other communities, followers of other beliefs in the same area where Francis lived, in the Spoleto Valley for example or also in southern France where Francis very much wanted to go. Why was he forbidden to go? The explanations found in Franciscan literature are not convincing, because they do not give reliable historical information. A last story found in the *Assisi Compilation,* AC 22, is an example of the ambiguity that pervades the account of Francis' identity as an epitome of a Catholic saint. The passage in question describes a very ill Francis who "blesses his brothers and shares bread with them."[23] We read:

> [...] he ordered loaves of bread to be brought to him. [...] he had them broken into many small pieces by one of the brothers. Taking them he offered each of the brothers a little piece telling them to eat all of it. Just as the Lord desired to eat with the apostles on the Thursday before his death. [...] One of the brothers kept a piece of that bread, and after the death of blessed Francis some people who tasted it were immediately freed from their illnesses.

This is an accurate description of the ceremony of the blessed bread that the Cathars practiced. It was their way to celebrate the Eucharist in memory of the last supper.[24] It is said that during persecutions the Cathars used to keep small pieces of the bread blessed by a *parfait*. It was called the *pain de Dieu*, God's

---
23   *Early Documents* II, 135.
24   Jean Duvernoy, *La religion des Cathars*. (Toulouse : Edition Privat, 1989), 212-216.

bread, and gave them spiritual strength. But the Cathars' world was a different one: it was the world that gave birth to the medieval demons, sorcerers and witches the Church imagined and fought against. Yet that different world was close, very close to Francis and his brothers. Would it be possible to find within the Cathars' world some interesting information or documents that could shed new light on the *Franciscan Question*?

From the broken mirror Francis' image comes forth dangerously unclear, vanishing into the fog of history, and so his brothers' images. Do we know who they really were? The *Assisi Compilation* is very convincing: we know nothing as yet.

CHAPTER TWO

THE MEDIEVAL CANONIZATION PROCESS

REALITY AND POLITICS. *VOX POPULI, VOX DEI?*

The canonization process is one of the most puzzling phenomena within the Catholic Church's structure. According to Aviad Klenberg, saints exist in all great religions such as Islam, Hinduism, Judaism, and Buddhism, and they are venerated by common people for their exceptional human qualities, but nowhere else is there such a painstaking effort meant to affirm and popularize sanctity as in Catholicism.[1] Klenberg points out that the medieval canonization process is not only an anomaly when compared to that of the other great religions: its entire procedure, with its complex mechanism torn between theological and legal issues, is unusual. In fact while it would make sense to examine the merit of an individual candidate for sanctity in open session and from the theological point of view, canonization is considered instead a legal case and discussed behind closed doors by a restricted circle of religious authorities, similar to an inquisition process:

> As in the inquisitorial process the judge's decision was final. [...] it might be interesting to see the saint as the positive counterpart of the heretic - a man characterized by excess and relentless tenacity. My point is simply to note that canonization was not an opportunity for free discussion on merit and character. It was a mostly technical examination of evidence. The judge's final aim was neither to reach the Truth in

---

1 Aviad Klenberg, *Procès de canonization au Moyen Âge; aspects juridiques et religieux* (École française de Rome, 2004), 7.

the theological sense of the word nor to develop a systematic profile of the perfect Christian saint. It was to reach a judicial decision.[2]

In 1201, with *Licet Apostolica Sedes,* Pope Innocent III established six requirements for the canonization process: first, the request for consideration of the case for a canonization had to originate from local initiative, that is, officially at the request of the local bishop with the support of the clergy and representative laity of his diocese; second, the Roman Curia, presided over by the Pope, designated a group of *postulators* who were charged to lead the preliminary investigation; third, after the *postulators'* report, the Curia named three commissioners, one of whom was normally the local bishop, to begin the official and more thorough inquiry on the holiness (*fama*) and miracles (*miraculi*) of the individual in question; fourth, an official *Life* (*vita*) of the postulated saint was commissioned whose very purpose was to attest to the *fama* and *miraculi* of the individual in question; fifth, the process of examination usually took place at or nearby the location of the postulated saint's tomb in order to attest to the performance of any miracles; sixth, the whole process was documented in writing by notaries whose written reports were then sealed and presented to the Curia for official examination and acceptance. The declaration of sanctity underwent a rigorous inquiry with the participation of eyewitnesses that had to testify under oath. The Roman Curia became evermore suspicious of the popular enthusiasm for a particular saint and was determined to exercise judicial control over sainthood.[3]

THE PAPAL WILL

Despite the published rules, at first the canonization process was a rather flexible tool in the hand of local bishops who followed people's desire to honor a particular meritorious individual. Through time, however, it changed from reflecting the religious need of local people to assuming the form of a rigidly judicial process controlled by a few cardinals and, especially, by the Pope himself. According to Vauchez, at the beginning canonization did not require a judicial procedure and often the decision was in the hands of local authorities: he confirmed that the process of canonization was at first simply the expression of a popular demand recognizing someone particularly respected and admired for his/her saintly life. But it soon happened that, in concomitance with the grow-

---

2 Ibid., 10.

3 André Vauchez, "Alle origini del processo di canonizzazione" *Diventare santo; itinerari e riconoscimenti della santità tra libri, documeni e immagini* a cura di Giovanni Morello, Ambrogio Piazzoni, Paolo Vian (Biblioteca Apostolica Vaticana, Events 1998), 54: "[...]la Santa Sede sottoponeva in tal modo il soprannaturale al controllo del diritto - che all'epoca era, non va dimenticato, la disciplina critica per eccellenza - all'interno di una procedura allo stesso tempo giuridica e giudiziaria, paragonabile a quella che si sarebbe diffusa qualche decennio più tardi durante la lotta contro l'eresia."

ing centralization of Church power, there was also an increase of papal control on the local Catholic communities both in Italy and abroad:

> With the Gregorian reform, the growth of papal prestige within the Church and within western Christendom led to an increase in the number of its interventions in the sphere of the cult of saints.[...] But there was no question of an obligation of a judicial order. [...] The approval of the Holy See was sought only in order to confer extra luster on certain cults. Things changed with the pontificate of Gregory VII (1073-85). [...][4]

During Gregory VII's pontificate the Pope himself was considered a candidate to sainthood inherently because of his position as representative of divine power.[5] There were certainly canonists who accepted the idea of sanctity reserved for the papal function but Vauchez points out that there was also strong reservation. He mentions that Rufinus in his Commentary on the *Decretum* concerning the sanctity of the Pope "says bluntly: *non loca sed vita et mores sanctum faciunt sacerdotem.*"[6] In any case, slowly but surely, the canonization process coincided with the expression of the papal will to gain control over his constituency. Thus we can justly say that at the beginning the canonization process followed the people's voice, as an expression of a divine will: *vox populi, vox Dei*. This situation, however, developed through the years according to a different religious and political environment: the *vox populi* became alienated from the *vox Dei*, the latter representing exclusively the Pope's material power to master particular circumstances that might evolve to undermine the Church's authority.[7] This trend evolved and developed centuries later in the declaration of *Papal Infallibility* during the council Vatican I on July 18, 1870. The Pope is now the only voice speaking for the Church's power.

The tendency toward centralization was already evident during the pontificate of Innocent III, who in *Cum secundum evangelicam veritatem* (3 April 1200), for the canonization of the Empress Cunegunda, stated that the Pope's *sublime iudicium* had to promote the celebration of a saint. Later in 1234 with the publication of the *Decretales Gregorii IX,* the decision of declaring sainthood was clearly reserved, at least theoretically, to papal authority. Vauchez reports that during the pontificate of Gregory IX we have the largest number

---

4 André Vauchez, *Sainthood in the later Middle Ages*, trans. by Jean Birrel (Cambridge: University Press, 1997), 22-23.

5 Ibid.: "[...] the Supreme Pontiff enjoyed a functional sainthood independent of his own merits to the extent that, as heir to the power of Peter, he exercised an authority both terrestrial and celestial" (p. 23).

6 Ibid., 24, n7. Trans.: *We recognize a priest by his saintly life and manners not by his social position.*

7 André Vauchez, *La sainteté en occident aux derniers siècles du moyen age* (Rome: École française de Rome Palais Farnese, 1981), 15 : "Dans les premiers siècles du christianisme, les seuls saints vénérés par l'Église, si l'on excepte la Vierge, Jean Baptiste et les Apôtres, furent les martyrs.[...] Leur sainteté, publiquement manifestée par leur mort et par leur persévérance dans la foi, a été aussitôt reconnue par les Églises auxquelles ils appartenaient: *vox populi, vox Dei.*"

of canonization processes.[8] There were compelling circumstances that urged the Pope to find new means to claim spiritual power in order to compensate for political weakness. This historical period presented several challenges to the Church's authority with the rise of imperial power and the surge of heretical movements. The Church badly needed support; thus, the two representatives and initiators of the new mendicant orders, Dominic and Francis, received the Pope's favors for their perceived ability to attract great numbers of followers. They were very useful to the church business; therefore, they were certain candidates to sanctity. While Francis' canonization, however, deserved full papal attention and speed from his death in 1226 to proclamation of sanctity in 1228, Dominic, deceased in 1221, had to wait for sainthood until 1234. We note then a fluctuation on the importance of being a saint, which varies according to material circumstances and to the degree of one's usefulness to the Church. The concept of usefulness became essential: it is in fact the principle upon which the Catholic doctrine developed. It transformed the original intent and organization of the *Fratres Minores* into a conventional order at the service of the Church's interests. Francis' life and the high drama played by Church representatives after his death still represent both a problem and an unsolved mystery. One has the impression that too much about Francis has been hidden or deformed by many who used his memory to their advantage. Greed for power and recognition has superseded the desire to emulate Francis' extraordinary insight of universal peace. In 1226 Pope Gregory IX certainly understood Francis' tremendous usefulness. He disregarded the process' rules that his predecessors had established and did not hesitate to push forward Francis' canonization with extraordinary celebrations and the building of the greatest basilica of his time in Assisi, meant to become the new spiritual center of Christianity.

SAINT ANTHONY, FRANCIS AND THE POPE

In a parallel case, Saint Anthony's canonization deserves attention because, as in Francis' proclamation of sanctity, Gregory IX did not follow the established rules for the canonization process, and the decision remained exclusively in his hands. At the time, the Pope was under pressure on two accounts: politically for the continuous interference of the Emperor in his domain and religiously for the increased danger of spreading heresy in Italian cities, particularly in the North. An important source of information in regard to Anthony's canonization is the *Vita prima* or *Assidua*, by an unknown author.[9] Roberto Paciocco

---

8 Vauchez, ibid., 295-297.

9 John Moorman, *A History of the Franciscan Order from its origin to the year 1517.* (Chicago: Franciscan Herald Press,1988), 290: "This First Life, generally known as *Assidua*, has been attributed to various writers including Thomas of Celano, John Pecham, S. Bonaventure, and others. It is now believed to have been the work of Thomas of Pavia, one of the hagiographers of the Order and author of a *Dialogus de Gestis Sanctorum Fratrum Minorum*. The Second Life, known as *Anonyma* was accredited

affirms that the *Assidua* has not received enough attention by historians when in fact it reflects the concrete problems affecting the Franciscan Order in the 1230s in the area of Padua.[10] The *Assidua* allows for a better understanding of the reasons for which Anthony's canonization process was pushed at full speed and did not follow the established protocol. Despites the *grande lacuna*,[11] the missing information for many years of Anthony's life, the *Assidua*'s author defined the important role played by Anthony in Padua's dioceses when he arrived there after a period of preaching in Romagna in 1223. Anthony participated in the official delegation sent to the Pope after the general chapter in Assisi in 1230 that asked the Pope to clarify the interpretation of Francis' Rule and Testament: on this occasion it was evident that Anthony was perfectly in tune with the new apostolic direction for the *Fratres Minores* that the Pope enunciated in his bull *Quo elongati*. Through Anthony's influence, Padua was supposed to become an important Catholic bastion enhanced by his great popularity; Anthony's preaching reinforced the apostolic program that The Holy See had promoted, inspired by the ruling of Lateran IV. An important part consisted in fighting heretical movements, even though, as we will see later, it did not seem that Anthony was particularly concerned about heresy. Nevertheless, at this point the Pope was determined to use Anthony's charisma to publicize and attract the population to Catholic religious practice. Augustine Thompson described the excitement shown among all kinds of people every time there was news of Anthony's preaching:

> When the news spread that the famous *Minorite* planned to preach at Padua, crowds streamed in from neighboring towns, castles, and villages, until the churches could no longer contain them. Anthony resorted to preaching in a wide-open field (*latissima pratorum spatia* - now known as the Prato della Valle).[12]

Anthony was not alone. Other representatives of local churches acted in unison, such as Bishop Giacomo Corrado and Giordano Forzatè, the very powerful head of the local Benedictine congregation, and several representatives of the best Paduan society, committed to the *correzione*, the correction of religious life in Padua. The intervention of these different personalities ignited

---

by the editors of the *Acta Sanctorum* to Julian of Speyer; but there is no real evidence for this.[...]some years later another life known as *Benignitas*, was written. Nicholas Glassberger, in the fifteenth century, ascribed it to Archbishop Pecham, but this is impossible since the legend was not written until after his time, though it contains some material which may well be authentic."

10 Roberto Paciocco, "'Nondum post mortem beati Antonii annus effluxerat': La santità romano-apostolica di Antonio e l'esemplarità di Padova nel contesto dei coevi processi di canonizzazione." *Il Santo*, 36 (1996): 113.

11 Gamboso in *Vita prima di Sant'Antonio o Assidua* (Padova,1981), 78 (chapter VIII dedicated precisely to *La grande lacuna*, [The great gap]).

12 Augustine Thompson, *Revival Preachers and Politics in Thirteenth-century Italy. The Great Devotion of 1233* (Oxford: Clarendon Press, 1992), 85.

a religious campaign between the end of 1229 and beginning of 1230. As the chronicler Rolandino affirms, when Anthony arrived in Padua he found himself *inter ceteros viros religiosos et iustos;*[13] with his arrival, the *Minores* participated in the religious reformation auspicated by the Pope.[14]

The local reaction to Anthony's death on June 13, 1231, demonstrated his great popularity. Two factions, one in Capo di Ponte and the other in the southern part of the city, claimed Anthony's remains provoking a series of disorders, for which the intervention of the *Minores*' general Giovanni Parenti was necessary, together with the city's high prelates as well as the *podestà*. Finally the body was buried in *S. Maria Mater Domini*. In this case public manifestations constituted proof of Anthony's popularity and the call for canonization was immediate. No doubt the local church and the *podestà* showed interest in transforming the city into a spiritual center dedicated to St. Anthony, which would have greatly enhanced the city's prestige while it counteracted the spreading of heresy and reinforced civil power against Frederic II's influence. Apparently there were two letters sent to the pope, one from local clerics and the other from civil authorities, in order to initiate the canonization process. Both letters, however, were lost and very little has come to us of the actual procedure. It is quite evident that, as in Francis' canonization, there was pressure from the Pope to have a quick proclamation of sanctity that could only benefit the diffusion of Catholic influence in an area that was religiously and politically troubled. Paciocco affirmed that in other canonization processes we find requirements and dispositions that were not requested for Anthony's demonstration of sainthood.[15] An example is the canonization of Giovanni Cacciafronte (1223-1224, deceased in 1183), bishop in Vicenza and previously *abate* (abbot) in Cremona, for whom it was necessary to complete two inquiries, one related to his activity in Vicenza and the other in Cremona. This one seems to be the first "double" commission, but there are others: the process for Dominic, in 1233, required a commission working in Bologna, but Gregory IX ordered also a supplemental inquiry in Toulouse and in Caleruega, the saint's place of origin. We do not see anything of the kind for Anthony, coming from Portugal to Romagna and last to Padua. His canonization process was held exclusively in Padua for everything concerning his life and deeds. This is quite an extraordinary situation considering that in the usual procedure adopted in the first half of the thirteenth century popes initiated two separate inquiries for someone *in*

---

13 Trans.: *among other just and religious men*. Rolandino, *Cronaca; vita e morte di Ezzelino Romano*. Ed. Flavio Forese (Fondazione Lorenzo Valla: Mondadori Editore, 2005), 118.

14 Paciocco, ibid., 115-116.

15 Ibid., 118-119 : "È da notare, però, che altre disposizioni pur riscontrabili in processi coevi non si rinvengono nella documentazione superstite per il *negotium* di Antonio."

odore di santità [16] who lived in different countries, such as in the process for the archbishop of Canterbury, Edmond of Abingdon, by Innocent IV in 1247.[17]

Contrary to other processes in the same period, but similarly to Francis' canonization described in the *Vita prima* by Tommaso da Celano, there has been no regular examination of Anthony's life and virtues required for sainthood. Both procedures, for Francis and Anthony, were based upon the saints' direct acquaintance with the Pope Gregory IX, who seemed to be personally interested in exalting their sanctity in putting it to work as soon as possible. To follow or not the established procedure was thus at the discretion of the Pope: in fact, differently from Anthony and Francis, Dominic and Clare who had also close personal relations with the Pope, were no exception and were not exonerated from having a regular inquiry to assess their moral quality.[18]

Francis' canonization was certainly the most extraordinary for the magnitude of the celebration and for the Pope's physical presence to the impressive ceremonial. In *Mira circa nos*, three days after the canonization, Gregory IX stressed his familiarity with Francis and left no doubt to the saint's high merit. For Anthony's case something similar happened though not as glamorously as for Francis. Anthony died 13 June 1231 and the Pope had already sent a first delegation with the required material before the 13 July that asked for *sollicitudo* in order to accelerate the *negotium* and proclaim his sainthood. After the first, there was a second and a third delegation, whose participants were important Paduan ecclesiastic personalities connected to the papal apostolic program. The third delegation finally succeeded in convincing the *Roman Curia* to approve the canonization: the Pope's familiarity with Anthony's activity was a determinant factor that accelerated the process. Concerning the Pope's alleged familiarity with the saint, as already mentioned, there is a memory of the meeting at the time Anthony went to Rome with a delegation to ask for Gregory IX' s decision on Francis' Rule and Testament, which resulted in the papal bull *Quo elongati*. But their relationship did not have the kind of intimacy that characterized Francis'closeness to Ugolino da Ostia, soon to become Gregory IX. Nevertheless, it shows an important aspect of Anthony's personality; in fact, contrary to Francis who fought until his last breath for the approval of his Rule when many, the Pope included, protested its excessive difficulty, Anthony was very much in agreement with the Pope's new interpretation of the Franciscan rule. Thus the proclamation of Anthony's sainthood was very useful to the papal apostolic program to encourage the mendicant order to preach for the good of the Church instead of following the original Franciscan program of social transformation. It is interesting to note that in the

---

16 *In odore di santità* is an Italian expression referring to someone who is a candidate to become saint.

17 Paciocco, ibid., 120.

18 André Vauchez, *La sainteté en Occident aux derniers siècles du Moyen Age*, 55.

Assidua the author mentions the perplexity of some of the cardinals, who did not approve of the excessive haste: a timely vision appeared in a dream to one of the undecided cardinals who was then convinced and ready to give his vote, reaching the necessary number of cardinals required for approving Anthony's canonization.[19]

The public declaration and ceremony was organized at the Pope's residence in Spoleto, 30 May 1232, and, right after, the commission was preparing for the first anniversary of Anthony's death in Padua. One day after the Spoleto ceremony, the Pope published the letter *Cum dicat Dominus* that announced the approved canonization. This letter differs from *Mira circa nos* in mentioning only slightly the person of Anthony and his merits contrary to the long list of biblical images illustrating Francis' personal moral qualities in *Mira circa nos*. The letter *Cum dicat Dominus* basically justified the canonization procedure by pointing out the local popular demand and the eagerness that the Paduan religious and civil authorities demonstrated. Moreover, using a *topos* typical in pontifical documents, Anthony was compared to a flame that had to be in everybody's view showing the brilliance of his charisma. A citation from Matthew 5, 15, in the *Cum dicat Dominus* stated: *nemo accendat lucernam et ponat eam sub modio sed super candelabrum ut omnes qui in domo sunt lumen videant*.[20] It continued to clarify the precise role of Anthony's canonization with an anti-heretical function *ad confundendam haereticam pravitatem et fidem catholicam roborandam*.[21] Just a few months after Anthony's death Gregory IX had applied the same images to the city of Padua itself in the letter to the *podestà*, to the *consilium* and to the people of Padua. In the letter, the Pope explained the procedure against Ezzelino da Romano who was ordered to present himself to the *Curia Romana* under threat of excommunication. We see then that Anthony's canonization overlapped with the political scenario: the Pope was trying to take advantage of Anthony's proclaimed sainthood with the intent of creating a barrier both to the heretical religious movement and to Ezzelino's growing ascendance in the Veneto region. Padua's citizens were encouraged to fight *contra dictum perfidum viriliter*[22] and to strengthen their faith in the Catholic Church by their devotion to the new saint.[23]

---

19 Paciocco, ibid., 125.

20 Trans.: *No one lights a lamp and puts it under a bushel but rather places it on a lampstand so that everyone in the house sees the light.*

21 Paciocco, ibid., 127-128. Trans.: *in order to destroy heretical perversity and to restore Catholic faith.*

22 Ibid., 128. Trans.: *Forcefully against the said deceitful person.*

23 In the summary-abstract section of *Il Santo*, 36 (1996): 426, Paciocco confirms: "[…] By the example of a *new* saint, who was *apostolic* according to the Roman Curia, it was also possible to consolidate the identity of Padua as a papal faithful town. […] the towns of Marches were giving signs of instability and Ezzelino da Romano was just beginning to cooperate with the Empire."

Ezzelino da Romano and the Emperor Frederik II

It remains to be seen what was the historical reality concerning heretical movements and the influence of Ezzelino da Romano in the region. To this day the person of Ezzelino and his involvement with heresy are not clear and his reputation varies greatly according to the origin of hagiographic sources. The city of Padua was well known for its orthodoxy given the high concentration of Catholic activity and the presence of important religious representatives, such as Giordano Forzatè, plus a list of individuals famous for being *in odore di santità* in the thirteenth century, all from wealthy local families strictly connected with the Church.[24] It is not the same for other cities in the Marches. The *retore* Boncompagno da Signa points out that concerning heresy "[...]*Verona claudicat, Vicentia iam victa succumbit, Tarvisium torpet, sola Padua in publico se defendit.*"[25] As a bastion of Catholic power Padua became naturally also a center of anti-Ezzelino hagiographic production manifesting the local ideology. In fact Ezzelino himself was tainted with accusation of heresy: Catholic orthodoxy and politics mixed and mingled under growing pressure from the Pope who was working actively for Ezzelino's elimination. At the time of Anthony's demise, Ezzelino was not yet in Padua but his strength was rapidly escalating in the region. In fact on 3 July 1230, after a period of adverse fortune, Ezzelino participated in the conquest of Verona together with the factions of Monticoli and Quattorviginti, previously at peace with the Pope. Together they deposed the Count Rizzardo of Sambonifacio and the papal legates, who during Ezzelino's absence had entered the city under the Count's protection. Ezzelino replaced the count with the more sympathetic Salinguerra Torelli and fought with his allies against the united cities of Mantova, Brescia, Vicenza and Padova.[26]

Ezzelino's shadow was already visible in Padua, although only on 29 March 1232, date of his alliance with the Emperor Frederik II, did he become a real threat to papal territorial ambition.[27] Ezzelino's decision, however, did not represent an alignment with the Ghibillines in opposition to the Guelphs and

---

24 Antonio Rigon, "Religione e politica," in *Nuovi Studi Ezzeliniani* a cura di Giorgio Gracco (Roma, Palazzo Borromini, 1992): 406-408. Rigon gives a list of celebrated Paduan saints in the 13th century, among which only Anthony deserved canonization: Luca Belludi, Elena Enselmini, Arnaldo da Limena, Giordano Forzatè, Beatrice d'Este, Compagno Ongarelli, Antonio il Pellegrino, Crescenzio da Camposampiero.

25 Ibid., 406. Trans.: *Verona is shaky, Vicenza, just surrendered, is falling, Tarvisium is struck motionless from fear, only Padua defends herself openly.*

26 Thompson, ibid., 65: "In Ezzelino's absence, the papal legates, James and Otto, had entered Verona accompanied by Count Richard of San Bonifacio. The count then made peace with the Montecchi and Quattorviginti parties. On returning to Verona, Ezzelino immediately drove out both Richard and the legates, thereby incurring the Church's wrath and excommunication."

27 Raoul Manselli, "Ezzelino da Romano nella politica italiana del sec. XIII," *Studi Ezzeliniani*, 45-47 (Roma: Palazzo Borromini, 1963), 42.

the papacy; in fact Ezzelino's family was traditionally Guelph.[28] Ezzelino's choice was purely political and strictly connected to the local tension between aristocratic families and the new class of merchants who actively fought for power in the region. For Ezzelino the alliance with Frederik II had the purpose of coordinating local interests and politics with the larger scope that coincided with the Emperor's plan. At the time the most important action was the consolidation of power in Verona, equally important to Ezzelino and to the Emperor for its strategic geographical position, an important point of communication between Italy and Germany.

The years 1230 and 1232 were crucial for creating the image of Ezzelino as a ruthless tyrant, whose alliance with the Pope's worst enemy transformed into a diabolic presence in the Veneto region. This image will grow darker and more ferocious in the years ahead. Ezzelino's alliance with the Emperor represented a formidable force that worked in unison and soon spread from Verona. It remained the most important Ezzelinian stronghold for the nearby cities and then for Padua, which was finally conquered in 1237.[29] Besides the political downfall for the Church due to Ezzelino's expansion, there was also the impossibility to fight heresy in all locations under the combined influence of Ezzelino and the Emperor. It must be said, however, that Ezzelino was never ideologically against the Church and in many occasions he showed consideration for it. Of course his respectful manner might have been simply a diplomatic ruse. Manselli mentions that Ezzelino had no opposition to John of Vicenza, the famous preacher who happened to be active near Verona in 1233 attracting a large audience. He actually went to listen to him and participated in a meeting in Paquara where John was proposing a peace treaty between the various local factions.[30] We are in 1233 at the time of the Alleluia movement that swept the region with renewed religious fervor and Ezzelino was aware of its irresistible force and influence on the population.[31] The ecclesiastical por-

---

28 Thompson, ibid., 64: "Traditionally, scholars have called the da Romano group the Imperial (or Ghibelline) party, since the da Romano held Verona in the name of Frederick. Their shifting alliance will show that the da Romano's imperial connection was more opportunistic than it was ideological. This group may be called the da Romano party for convenience, even though its different members had a variety of interests that did not always correspond with those of that family."

29 Manselli, ibid., 48-50.

30 Ibid., 43-44.

31 The new energy given by the mendicant friars to popular preaching had prepared the way for the impressive manifestation of the Alleluia movement. We must consider that the 1233 Alleluia phenomenon besides being religious had a highly political tone that was of course encouraged by the Church. See Thompson, ibid., 98-99: "Observers of the Alleluia tell us that a preacher was heard 'by all classes, ages and sexes' [...]. Even nobles and wealthy merchants would turn out to hear a celebrated preacher. The highborn Federico Visconti came to Bologna specifically to hear and touch St. Francis. An irreligious magnate like the vicious Ezzelino da Romano took care to show up for at least those of John of Vicenza's sermons that touched on the politics of his region. [...] when the thrust of the preaching touched on peace-making and politics, as it often did in early thirteenth-century Italy, self-interest dictated their attendance."

trait of Ezzelino is certainly not flattering. It is, however, evidently biased, because the opposition had a unilateral vision and had high interests at stake in the Paduan region.[32] Diabolic nature was detected in anything or anyone undermining papal influence. For an honest historian it is often difficult to recognize who is the tyrant, considering that history is written by the last one who remains in power regardless of how power was won.[33] Ezzelino is a complex case that, if seen as a brutal oppressor from one side, it acquires new light and intent when we switch to a different view. Carlo Polizzi, for example, analyzed the socio-economic environment in the Veneto region in the thirteenth century. He found Ezzelino at the crossroad between the historical developments from aristocratic predominance to the growing expansion of the mercantile class. His analysis brings to the conclusion that Ezzelino's political action was in reality most necessary and appropriate in order to help an orderly change in the region's social dynamic. Polizzi has a collective vision of historical circumstances in which Ezzelino's violent repressions had their motivation in the extreme tension between the old aristocratic power of local families and the social dialectic that the rising new class of merchants represented.[34]

In any case Gregory IX had to combat a double enemy: his traditional enemy the Emperor, coupled with Ezzelino's powerful hold on the local families, and the heresy evermore intense in northern Italy. With Anthony's canonization, the Pope intended that the most Catholic city in the north, Padua, would become a Catholic stronghold, a place of respite and devotion just as the proclamation of Francis' sainthood had done in central Italy. As mentioned before, at that time it was practically impossible for the Pope to counteract the spread of heretical movements wherever Frederick II or Ezzelino exercised political power. Both the Emperor and Ezzelino were not interested in a religious war; their goal was the socio-political organization of their domain. Thus heretics in their territories who belonged to any particular movement (Cathars, Waldensians or others) enjoyed great freedom and could organize themselves without problems. But let's not forget that there was a real and good reason for

---

[32] Ezzelino is still today a mysterious character, and we do not have sufficient documentation for a fair judgment. In his work *The Cathars* (Blakewell Publishing, 1998, 2007), 185-186, Malcolm Lambert argues: "[...] he was indifferent to excommunication and papal exhortation or threat, though he recognized Church authority [...]; formally correct in his relationship with the Church in his territories, he even exerted a curious fascination over his churchmen, for which they were rebuked by Innocent IV. He quietly appeared among the mass audience of John of Vicenza recognizing that, for some months, John was a true political force, accepted the reconciliations John imposed, then resumed his political and military strategy as the enthusiasm for the Alleluia faded. [...] For all his formal acceptance of the traditional rights of the Church as he saw them, his culture was profoundly non-Christian. His passion for astrology, his interest in magic, his relations with Arabs are straws in the wind. [...]"

[33] The chronicler Rolandino da Padova is the main source for Ezzelino. Unfortunately the writer is one of Ezzelino's enemies. He represents the Guelph tradition most hostile to Ezzelino.

[34] Carlo Polizzi, *Studi e documenti Ezzeliniani. Ezzelino da Romano. Signoria territoriale e comune cittadino* (Comune di Romano D'Ezzelino: Sezione Cultura e Ricerca Storica, 1989), 78-79.

the large success of different religious interpretations considering the material greed, corruption and violence that characterized the Church's activity. Let's also note that the word heresy became a blanket statement, a cover-up for anything that was contrary or not completely in agreement with the papal will. The Pope was more concerned about the people's spiritual beliefs; his concern, however, and the concern of his most faithful followers, was all but spiritual. It was based upon material power and political interest not unlike Ezzelino's drive for predominance. Actually, Ezzelino's politics might have made more sense because it seemed to be more in tune with the time's natural changes in social interaction, while the Pope simply imposed his will in anachronistic fashion; he forced the truth with unrealistic expectations and deformed the intention of the most pure interpreters of the Catholic religion. We said before that this period saw the greatest number of canonized saints, that is, the Church was in absolute need to use the example of "Christian perfection" in order to win its religious wars.[35]

THE POWER OF CANONIZATION

Canonization became a powerful tool for impressing Catholic masses with a magnificent, dazzling display of power symbolic of Church's spiritual greatness, thus attracting many to be part of such greatness while abiding by the principles dictated by the Pope. We can imagine that both Francis and Anthony would have strongly disapproved of the pompous celebration planned after their deaths in honor of their lives. According to Vauchez, "the founders of the Mendicant orders had been guarded, if not hostile, towards external manifestations of sainthood." He continued to explain that in the *Chronica XXIV generalium*, Francis appeared strongly against miracles and the exploitation of the deeds of saints "in order to derive honor and glory for ourselves."[36] Jordan of Giano wrote that Francis did not appreciate hagiographical tales that exalted someone's noble actions and "he forbade anyone to read it and pushed it away, saying 'let everyone gain glory with his own passion and not that of others.'"[37] Nothing was more contrary to the Pope's design than Francis' words. But Vauchez also affirmed that after Francis' death, "The reticence of

---

[35] Vauchez argues: "We find traces in the bull of canonization, where popes celebrated, with much recourse to biblical imagery, the assistance of the saints in the battle against the heresy. Here, too, the rhetorical formula is not entirely remote from reality, since the majority of those who were recognized as saints by Rome at this period, from St. Homobonus to St. Peter Martyr, were fierce opponents of the Cathars, and many towns and regions had been recovered for Catholicism by their action and miracles: St. Dominic in Languedoc and Anthony of Padua in Venetia, John Bonus in the Romagna and, lastly, St. Francis himself, indirectly but no less effectively. To combat dualistic doctrines and demonstrate to the masses the superiority of orthodoxy, the Church was in dire need, in the first two-thirds of the thirteen century, of Christian perfection." *Sainthood in the later Middle Ages*, 112.

[36] Ibid., 115.

[37] Ibid.

the Friars Minors toward the cult of the saints was, however, short lived,"[38] as we can see following the history of the Franciscan Order.

For what concerns the fight against heresy both Francis and Anthony did not seem interested in taking a clear stand; the lack of documentation allows for different interpretations. Ironically, heresy seemed to be exclusively a papal problem: for very different reasons all other parties in this historical game, Francis, Anthony, Ezzelino and Frederick II, did not seem to be interested.

Francis was certainly a unique case. He never mentioned the word heresy, seemingly unaware of its existence, even though he was active in a region filled with a variety of heretical communities. Francis defined the brothers who did not follow the rule as *non Catholic,* and this was as far as he could go; not far enough for assuming his clear stand against heresy. He was probably keenly aware of the danger of being misinterpreted by the papal curia. Suppose he was actually in contact with the so-called heretics, living with them as with others: heretics were in Orvieto, Spoleto and Assisi, in the whole area where Francis and his brothers operated. Raoul Manselli confirmed the absence of references to heretics in Francis' documents: "Una constatazione [...] si impone ed è l'assenza di riferimenti specifici e diretti di qualsiasi tipo ad eretici o a fedi e fatti ereticali, negli scritti di Francesco d'Assisi."[39] In his article, however, he strived to demonstrate that Francis was in fact against heresy and took as example *Il Cantico delle Creature*; he interpreted it as Francis' hymn to the world in contraposition to the Cathars' negative vision of existence.[40]

Concerning Anthony, Vergilio Gamboso specified that the saint did not share the current violent ideology against heresy. In his writings and hagiography we cannot find any involvement with anti-heretical papal politics.[41] Merlo agreed explaining in detail that the fame of Anthony's activity and preaching against heresy was posthumous, due to the process of transformation from chronicle to hagiography.[42] Anthony, *instancabile martello degli eretici,*[43] became a stereotype much later after his death. The *Assidua,* considered the

---

38 Ibid., 115.

39 Raoul Manselli, "San Francesco e l'eresia" *Annali della Facoltà di Lettere e Filosofia. Università di Siena,* 5 (1984): 51-70, 52. Trans.: *It is necessary[...] to realize the absence of specific references direct to any heresy or heretical movements in the writings of Saint Francis of Assisi.*

40 Ibid., 52-53. Mentioning the *Cantico delle creature* Manselli affirms "[...]vuole essere l'antitesi, sentito come spirito unitario e come forza di coesione, alla lotta inerente alla concezione catara [...]" Trans.: *(The Cantico) wants to be the antithesis, a unified spirit and a cohesive force, against the struggle implicit in Cathar's interpretation.*

41 Vergilio Gamboso, *Antonio di Padova.Vita e spiritualità* (Padua, Edizioni Messaggero,1995), 24: "Antonio visse in quest'era di rovente crociatismo, senza tuttavia condividerlo. Mai nella sua vita, nei suoi scritti, nel suo *miracoliere* cogliamo echi di un'ideologia che davvero faceva a pugni con la spiritualità del Vangelo."

42 Grado Giovanni Merlo, "La santità di Antonio e il problema degli eretici" *Il Santo,* 36 (1996): 187-202.

43 Trans.: *the tireless hammer against heretics.*

most reliable biographic source for Anthony's life, reports one case in which Anthony is in Rimini. Realizing the presence of many heretics, *multi heretica pravitate delusi*,[44] he gathered the population and began to preach and assert the spiritual truth of orthodoxy, with immediate effect of instant conversions. From this unique information on Anthony's preaching against heresy in *Assidua*, the Rimini event was elaborated upon and enhanced into an anti-heretical mode in the *Benignitas*, the next biographic source, written perhaps by John Peckham, that attributed to Anthony a strong intent to eradicate all heretics *(pro viribus expugnare, funditus destruere atque radicitus extirpare)*. This time Anthony was not only preaching in Rimini, but also in Toulouse and Milan. Anthony's alleged revulsion of heresy grew in the *Rigaldina* with more tales giving way to the *Actus/Fioretti* that celebrated Anthony's miracles in a variety of fantastic performances.[45] Merlo concluded that, despite the fascinating literature on Anthony's anti-heretical activity, very little can be assumed to be a concrete historical reality. The hagiographic tales were meant to enhance all the aspects useful to the success of the Church's politics. The transformation of Anthony's reputation, however, in *martello degli eretici* was already implicit in the event of his canonization. Regardless of Anthony's true feeling and action, the Roman Curia had a very clear agenda. At this point in the history of the Franciscan Order, Anthony had an important role due to his great influence on the population combined with his declared orthodoxy that was firmly ingrained in the papal apostolic program.

All things considered, with all the similarities related to the canonization process, Anthony was to be contrasted with Francis, whose memory for the Pope was probably an embarrassment, soon to become a real and growing problem more than an example to imitate. Anthony's sainthood became necessary for the Pope's religious and political agenda. There was no question that his canonization was strictly connected with local and regional politics directed also to eliminate Ezzelino's power: the supposed action of Anthony against heresy was a later hagiographical construction that reflected papal will.[46] In his article Merlo cited Antonio Rigon who stated that Anthony belonged to a category of friars representatives of an international *minoritismo*

---

44 Trans.: *many deceived by perverse heresy.*

45 Ibid., 190-192.

46 Vauchez in "Attorno a Sant'Antonio di Padova, Conclusioni a Vite e vita di Antonio di Padova" *Atti del convegno internazionale sulla agiografia antoniana* (Padova, 29 maggio-1 giugno 1995), 140-141: "Penso che dobbiamo certo interpretare la rapidità della canonizzazione di sant'Antonio senza dubbio come un fenomeno legato a delle considerazioni di politica religiosa locale e regionale. Era allora necessario per il papato dare forza a Padova come baluardo della fede cattolica nel Veneto e nella Marca Trevigiana in un momento in cui la Chiesa si sentiva minacciata dall'azione di Ezzelino e dai suoi alleati [...] Per finire vorrei aggiungere solo due parole per sottolinerae l'importanza di quanto è stato detto a proposito dell'azione di Antonio di fronte all'eresia. È stato dimostrato, mi sembra, in modo indiscutibile che la sua predicazione non era antiereticale in primo luogo. L'espressione *martellus haereticorum* è un'aggiunta a posteriori che non si trova nell'Assidua."

padovano, developed far away from Umbria, and from Francis, with strong ties to the Roman Curia. Contrary to Francis, Anthony was perfectly in tune with the new apostolic direction so dear to the Pope. Despite the lack of evidence for Anthony's direct political involvement, it is clear instead that right from the beginning Anthony's cult had a highly charged political motivation in harmony with Gregory IX's desire to exterminate at the same time Ezzelino and heresy.[47] As the danger of Ezzelino's expansion in the region increased, Anthony's sanctity and his reputation of *martellus haereticorum* also grew in a myriad of miraculous tales. Padua, reflecting Anthony's spirituality, was transformed into a blessed city where the crusade against Ezzelino promoted by Alexander IV was going to be played until the city was freed from the tyrant. With little resemblance to the real Anthony, the saint was now a powerful entity, *pater Paduae*, father of Padua the *New Jerusalem*, a city that had become the symbol for the triumph of a militant Church. At first restricted to local devotion, Anthony's fame expanded in a national cult that was destined to attract international renown.

In parallel with the glamorous success of canonization stories such as Francis' celebration and Anthony's *negotium*, the Church never acknowledged countless individualities deserving recognition for their saintly lives. In many instances popular saints, celebrated locally by collective choice, were not useful enough to the Church's politics, thus a canonization process was not considered. On the other hand the Church did not want to antagonize the population by fighting established local beliefs: with a "silent rejection"[48] the Church simply ignored popular cults it did not consider important to its political power. *Vox populi* will never coincide again with *vox Dei*; the latter exclusively expressed *vox Ecclesiae* imposing its will. One might suspect that deep at its root such practice showed the Church's lack of self-confidence in its own values attempting to compensate with a display of power; the will to influence the population at large in order to gain and maintain political and material predominance has been astonishing throughout the Church's history. Aviad Klenberg reminded us:

> The Catholic Church alone developed various mechanisms whereby the hierarchy seeks to examine and either endorse or disqualify emerging cults. It is very easy for students of western culture not to realize how extraordinary this attempt to regulate the cult of saints is. Medievalists are so conditioned to expect the expansionist - totalitarian one might say - attitude to religious matters that we tend to relate to the so-called papal monarchy that its claim to control the cult of the saints comes as no surprise. But surprising it is. [49]

---

47 Merlo, *La santità di Antonio e il problema degli eretici*, 198-199.
48 Vauchez, ibid., English translation, 413.
49 Klenberg, ibid., 7.

If for nothing else, the Church must be commended for the diplomatic shrewdness her representatives cultivated that allowed for her survival in the most daring situations. The medieval process of canonization is the product of the keen attention and concern with which the Church exercised a clever politics directed toward an ever-growing influence at every social level. We can conclude with Grado Merlo that indeed sainthood was and is a formidable tool in the hands of papal power and of all its followers.[50]

---

50 Merlo, ibid., "La santità è un formidabile strumento nelle mani del papato e delle forze che ad esso fanno riferimento,"199.

CHAPTER THREE

SAINTS AND DEMONS IN MEDIEVAL SPACE

THE SACRED AND THE PROFANE
MARGHERITA DA CORTONA

Exploring the world of medieval saints and demons is a bit like finding oneself in the "foresta oscura," the dark forest of Dante's memory: loud voices, muffled voices, arrogant or sweet, blistering or soothing, they all mix in an impossible cacophony. Direct sources are lacking, historical proofs are absent, yet we still write, think, imagine and interpret the few documents describing that remote time during which our ancestors molded our present. This writing celebrates the untold lives of women of past ages, the forgotten, unnamed women without history who nursed the famous and infamous protagonists of our civilization. It reaches back to those unknown women, the real building blocks of our society, who disappeared in the dark, unexplored space of the medieval era.

Taking into account that during the Middle Ages oral communication was prevalent, written documents represent only a minimal part of the space in which people lived: hence, there is a stark contrast between the physical and psychological spaces in which religious, political, social happenings mingled and influenced one another and the available written documents that tell us a tiny fraction of past social reality.[1] In reasoning that each document gives an

---

1 See Paul Zumthor, *La mesure du monde. Représentation de l'espace au Moyen Age*. (Edition du Seuil: 1993), 363. : « [...] du fait que l'objet étudié appartient à une civilisation où l'oralité des transmissions prédomina - de beaucoup - sur l'écriture [...] Avant le XVI siècle, il serait irréaliste, de la part de l'historien, de ne point dissocier, dans les cultures européennes les idées de texte et d'écrit. » Trans. « [...] because the object under consideration belonged to a civilization in which oral transmission was predominant ... in European culture before the sixteenth century it would be unrealistic for a

incomplete reading, the well-known problem is that the best legal writing that would seem to clarify a specific historical situation can be deceiving. Another manuscript might come out to tell us the contrary or to significantly modify the first one. We have then a variety of literary texts, hagiography, legal contracts, personal letters and papal bulls, all waiting to be placed in the right context and to be given the correct meaning in the historical tapestry: before being allowed to testify as witnesses of historical truth, they are nothing else but literature. It is up to the historian to elect which one is telling the truth.

In his introduction to *Cities of God* Augustine Thompson stated: "Shared religion is shared behavior as well as space."[2] He went on to explain his intention to describe the Italian thirteenth-century city in all its components, by examining the day-by-day life of ordinary citizens. He mentioned: "Herbert Grundmann first suggested that high medieval heresy, the mendicants, and women's mysticism all formed part of a single whole and deserved more attention."[3] He understood the necessity to explore the entire city's spatial dimension including popular religion and local beliefs that were strictly interconnected to orthodox Christianity and often occupied large spaces in Italian communities. From these large spaces, where ancient local traditions survived maintaining a quasi-independence from ecclesiastic rules, grew manifestations of intense religiosity often opposed to official orthodoxy. At the same time we cannot forget that in Italy, in the past and in the present, as in no other nation, religion is strictly connected with politics and economy. No saint or mystic existed whose activity did not play into the hands of political or economical interests in favor of or against involved individuals. Thus, we have a very intricate space that does not allow the historian to consider one element to the exclusion of others. The life of a saint in medieval hagiography was only one facet in a complex structure that involved local politics, popular belief and miraculous spectacular events combined with the ever-present influence of the Roman Curia. It took centuries before the spacious, polyvalent richness of the medieval text could transform itself in the solitary corner occupied by the modern reader, alone in front of a black and white page or examining medieval documents profoundly disincarnated from their original environment.

Despite all the differences, however, in the lifestyle dictated by modern technology and the difficulty, sometimes the impossibility, to perceive the reality of our past, we might keep in mind that, all things considered, the desire for personal accomplishment and the power game needed to survive and succeed

---

historian not to be able to separate the ideas derived from the social space (texte) and from the written documents."

2   Augustine Thompson, *Cities of God. The Religion of the Italia Communes 1125-1325*. (Penn State University Press, 2005), 8.

3   Ibid., 1.

either in the material or spiritual world have been and are always the building blocks of human experience at any historical time. Men and women went through life asserting their roles in society with a variety of personal struggles just as it happens today. But in the twelfth and thirteenth centuries, a particular reaction to the social environment provoked among women a unique phenomenon that spread all over Europe, taking multiform shapes according to local customs. The common denominator was women's need to gather together to share their living spaces and organize their daily lives in common activities. A small fraction of these women shaped the religious beliefs of Italian communities and remained in Italian history as vivid examples of Christian sanctity. The rest of them, invisible to official history, went their way probably just trying to survive. Were all the women, who participated in the communities, dedicated to religious pursuit or were there other important elements, more or equally compelling that pushed women to search for support among others in a community life?

No one can establish for sure if at the beginning there was a clear religious connotation attached to the laywomen's communities. In *The Laity in the Middle Ages,* Vauchez mentioned Father Meersseman as a unique case of "intellectual probity as a historian" because, "debunking century old myths," he did not hesitate to contradict common assumptions among scholars.[4] Vauchez recognizes the reality of Meersseman's interpretation:

> Father Meersseman has correctly situated this process in the context of the vast movement of association which characterized this period and whose varied terminology was so incisively studied by the late father Michaud-Quantin [...] The historian is thus confronted with a swarm of communitarian initiatives in the professional, political, and even military sectors, among which, given the available documentation, it is difficult to identify with certainty the ones which were specifically confraternities of devotion.[5]

Meersseman points out precisely the extreme complexity of the medieval environment in which a variety of elements intersected and where religiosity was only one of them. In his work *Ordo Fraternitatis, Confraternite e pietà dei laici nel medioevo,*[6] Meersseman explained in details the historical circumstances. He distinguished between a *pia confraternita,* a religious community and an *associazione,* a community whose purpose was completely profane. Even when a letter from the Pope was available as documentation, it would not be enough to truly understand whether the association was for *salus ani-*

---

4   André Vauchez, *The Laity in the Middle Ages. Religious Beliefs and Practices.* Ed. Daniel Bornstein, Trans. Margery Schneider (Notre Dame, IN, and London: University of Notre Dame Press, 1987), 108.

5   Ibid., 110-111.

6   Gilles Gerard Meersseman, *Ordo Fraternitatis, Confraternite e pietà dei laici nel medioevo.* (Roma : Herder Editrice, 1977).

marum, for the salvation of souls. Meersseman gave the example of a letter written by Gregorio Magno in 599; the letter addressed to the bishop of Naples ordered him to protect the corporation of the *saponai* (soap-makers) against the Emperor's lieutenant. The letter showed that corporations either religious or commercial, established by people of a particular trade, in this case making soap, had the same statute, the same obligations and penalties for its members. Thus even though the Church was always involved in all ventures, it is difficult to establish today which one among the hundreds of existing corporations was in fact of a religious nature.[7] The Church had a capillary influence in all matters, material or spiritual, and its main scope was to counteract the Emperor's influence impeding its expansion. The same observation is valid for Meersseman in regard to the literary societies that were often entitled to the Virgin Mary or to a popular saint: he specified that to adopt a patron saint was not enough to count a lay association among the pious confraternities; many commercial corporations adopted a patron saint.[8] Meersseman's work helped to understand the complexity of the social structures. In the Middle Ages working in groups and associations, later called guilds, must have been most normal compared to the present: we are used to individual tasks and often not even capable to work in a group. Oral communication was more valuable than a written agreement: today it is the opposite. There are other differences worth mentioning: the language that defined specific events or states of being changed meaning through the centuries and came to us somewhat deformed. Meersseman carefully analyzed the change in meaning from Latin to the vulgar, popular language; he expressed preoccupation for being able to convey the precise content. For example the word *religiosus*, was applied to all devout Christians without any suggestion of religious status.[9] Or, in another example, the word *poenitentes* defined people who were forced *to* penitence because they were guilty of some misbehavior, while the voluntary penitents growing in number in the twelfth century were similar to *conversi or religiosi viri*, often men who had enough means to live comfortably and decided to spend the rest of their life in devotion. The *mulieres devotae* were respectable women who chose a domestic monastic life versus the institutionalized enclosure in a monastery. The linguistic aspect with the etymologic origin of words used from the tenth and eleventh to fourteenth centuries, going from Latin to vulgar, constitutes a field of study in its own. The definitions that applied to the different role

---

7   Ibid., 9 : Meersseman writes: « Per poter affermare che una società aveva come scopo principale *la salus animarum* non basta infatti che il documento che ci rivela la sua esistenza sia una lettera del papa che la prese sotto la sua protezione, come quella con cui nel 599 Gregorio Magno ordinò al vescovo di Napoli di difendere contro il luogotenente dell'imperatore la corporazione dei saponai[…]»

8   Ibid. "…per poter annoverare un'associazione laicale fra le pie confraternite, non basta che essa abbia adottato un santo patrono: lo adottavano pure molte corporazioni di arte e mestieri."

9   Ibid., 218-219, n.1.

of men and women were in place since the very beginning of the Church and with the change in customs acquired new meaning added to the original, thus making the interpretation of documents ever more confusing. When women began associating together in a life style that was soon motivation for critique and concern, the definition *mulieres devotae* slowly transformed into *pinzocchere, beghine or mantellate* with pejorative meanings; this shows the change in public perception that went from approval to suspicion. It happened in concomitance with the stricter discipline the Church imposed upon women's associations. There is in fact a clear progression toward increasing pressure from clerical authorities that expected women to follow religious rules. Pope Honorius in 1216 had endorsed the beguines' lifestyle even though in 1215 the Fourth Lateran Council had formally prohibited new religious communities; in 1233, however, Gregory IX, while accepting the beguines' communal life, determined that only enclosed beguines could have papal support. As time went by the situation for the beguines became ever more ambiguous and in parallel their lives were vulnerable to the local interpretation of individual clerics, until in 1311 when Pope Clement V, with a sharp turn in the evolution of language meanings, decided to call them heretics.[10]

Laywomen formed at first small, loosely organized groups, and soon they attracted an ever-greater number of women from the working class, the rich middle class, the merchants, and from nobility. As Meersseman explained, one of the main reasons for the multiplication of non-enclosed women penitents was probably economic. Many of these women attracted by the lay-pietism current at the time, along with the beginning of Gregorian reform, did not possess an adequate dowry to enter a regular traditional monastery.[11] The beginning of the thirteenth century saw the solution of this social problem with the organization of *beguinages* or *courts* in northern Europe and in Italy with the hospices for penitents. These communities did not accept any of the traditional religious rules, so that the *Memoriale propositi fratrum et sororum de Penitentia in domibus propriis exsistentium* was generally adopted. It was an older regulation for men and women who were dedicated to practice penance at their own home: it was afterward modified and restructured in 1221 by Ugolino da Segni.[12]

The economical and political situation in Italy in the twelfth and thirteenth centuries did affect greatly people's attitudes toward religiosity, and it is very possible that economy and socio-politics could be the prevalent aspect of the

---

10 Kate Crawford Galea, "Unhappy Choices: Factors that Contributed to the Decline and Condemnation of the Beguines" *On Pilgrimage, The Best of Vox Benedictina 1984-1993*. (Winnipeg, Manitoba: Hignell Printing, 1994), 505-518.

11 Meersseman, 282.

12 Ibid., 265-283.

social dynamic. In the twelfth-century Italian society had manifest symptoms of internal crisis among the regular traditional religious orders and also between clerics and laics. According to Anna Benvenuti Papi, regular religious institutions, particularly in central and northern Italy, such as the Benedictines, Vallombrosans and Camaldolesi, were declining at the same time that the decadent rural aristocracy was disappearing, because of the changed dynamic of economic production that was now concentrated in the cities.[13] Italian communes developed rapidly as soon as they acquired independence from imperial dominance, even though, as Thompson explains: "The German monarchs did not formally acknowledge the cities' *de facto* independence or legitimacy until the Peace of Costanza in 1183, and even then only grudgingly."[14] Italian cities were able to win control from imperial rule in the 1100s, but some bishops who had been appointed by the German emperors were not in agreement with the new government. They often succeeded in being able to work together; the conflict, however, between the commune and clerics "could escalate into violence." Thompson explains:

> At Piacenza ecclesiastical and secular authorities clashed in 1204 and the Piacentine clergy abandoned their city for three years. At Bologna in 1193, where Bishop Girardo di Ghisello Scannabecchi had been elected city executive, the four consuls of the commune fell moot with the Bishop-*podestà*. A faction developed around the bishop. Soon communal and Episcopal mobs fought in the streets, torching each other's houses.[15]

In any case, either with cooperation or without, the communal government developed sharing space with the ecclesiastics and so it happened that, as in Bologna, sacred and secular space mingled and often were not separately recognizable: "They were an integrated whole."[16] Each town then had its own particular configuration that clerics or laymen could alternatively influence according to local, political circumstances. During the religious revival called *Alleluia* of 1233, the Mendicants preachers, the most popular orders at the time, Franciscans and Dominicans, organized peacemaking between fighting civil factions and instituted, in agreement with the communes, a religious ritual, the *Kiss of Peace* that became part of cities' statutes.

Thompson pointed out the strict interdependence between civil and religious practices and laws. A good example is the function of the baptistery in the city life: "For thirteenth-century Italians the religious heart of the commune

---

13 Anna Benvenuti Papi, *In castro poenitentiae. Santità e società femminile nell'Italia medieval*. (Roma: Herder Editriice, 1990), 114.
14 *Cities of God*, 104.
15 Ibid., 104-105.
16 Ibid., 105.

was not the cathedral but the baptistery [...]. The attachment to the baptistery was almost physical, certainly experiential."[17] The baptistery in many Italian cities still stands witness to the power of the religious institution. Thompson, however, reminds:

> The baptistery was not merely the site of baptism [...] was the shrine of the republic. In 1262, after Vicenza had thrown off the yoke of the tyrant Ezzelino da Romano, one of the restored republican government's first acts was to commission the construction of a new baptistery. They placed it in the piazza between the cathedral of Saint Mary and the Episcopal palace. The space around the baptistery was sacred: no executions might be performed there. Frescoes on the outside of the baptistery, as at Verona, commemorated important and sometimes frightful, events in city history. [...] [18]

The baptistery was one of the main ingredients in Christian life; it signified the soul's spiritual rebirth. It was the first step toward a religious life devoted to the Catholic Church. But at the same time the baptistery was also the symbol of state power, the place where the *carroccio*[19] and the military banners were kept. In the sacred space created around the baptistery that we could still physically experience today, Church and State with all their particular interests intertwined. The Church's influence, however, was pervasive and in the long run overrode the citizens' efforts to establish civic laws and completely infiltrated and saturated all available space. Slowly the preachers were able to convince the cities' consuls to enact anti-heresy regulations. With local variations and despite the effort to separate and distinguish civil administration and Church administration, it was in practice not possible to avoid the Church's influence upon civic affairs: a situation that fluctuated through the centuries, but never changed in Italian society. Using censorship and propaganda, the Church was able to penetrate Italian culture at its deepest level so that even in modern time the Italian state itself has absorbed within its judicial system articles of laws once promulgated by Episcopal authority.[20] There has never been separation between Church and State in Italian society. Thompson argues that in the late thirteenth century:

> The growing division of civil and ecclesiastic jurisdictions paradoxically led the commune to cultivate an ever more sacred ethos for itself. [...] Secularized communes needed their own divine legitimacy. They sought it in heaven, invoking the protection

---

17 Ibid., 27.

18 Ibid., 27-28.

19 *Il carroccio* is emblematic of the encroachment between Church and State being a war chariot, a rectangular platform adorned with the city banners. On the chariot dressed as an altar priests would hold services before the battle, while trumpeters encouraged soldiers to fight.

20 L. Troncelliti, "All'ombra della Controriforma. Dal *Discorso* di Paleotti alla *Ricotta* di Pasolini." *Italica. Journal of the American Association of Teachers of Italian*, Vol. 84. No.2-3 (Summer/Autumn 2007), 548-555.

of new patron saints and on earth, saturating their laws, assemblies, and communal institutions with sacred rhetoric, symbolism, and ritual.[21]

For example the Italian republics were never in favor of crusades, but, despite the commune's lack of enthusiasm, the Bolognese chronicle reported that "two thousand" crusaders left Bologna in 1188 and many went east after the fall of Damietta in 1219: the Christian spirit won over civil distaste for the crusades and the city accepted to send its men to combat for the Church. Another example is the political struggle of Padua against Ezzelino that in 1259 became a religious war:

> Ezzelino was Goliath the Philistine; little Padua was David: God gave the weak victory over the mighty. The rhetoric of divine favor and holy war implied that God and his saints led the commune in battle. [...] During the early to mid-1220s, there was no greater danger to northern republican liberties than the tyrant Ezzelino da Romano, vicar of the Emperor Frederick II. The Holy war against Ezzelino and Frederick revealed new celestial friends of the communes.[22]

In this climate of complete encroachment of sacred and profane space in which seculars and clerics competed for divine favors, the continuous production of new patron saints in every Italian city was necessary. During the thirteenth and fourteenth centuries, lay communities of men and women were fertile ground for the cultivation of this necessary element and the production was extraordinarily abundant among women. Naturally, for the unavoidable dualistic bent of human minds, wherever there were saints there were demons. In the medieval space there were plenty of them sprouting from people's imagination, pullulating every corner, willing to communicate and perfectly visible in plain daylight for almost everybody who wanted to see them.

Strangely enough sometimes medieval demons seemed to be all in favor of the Church's doctrines and justified themselves with sophisticated reasoning. Barbara Newman mentioned some cases recounted in Jacques de Vitry's *Exempla*:

> Jacques tells of another demon who "used to present the truth willingly and often through the mouth of a person he had entered, and expounded many things from the Divine Scriptures." Conjured by a Holy man, the demon is asked why he preaches the truth, being the enemy of truth. He replies that his preaching is meant to harm those

---

21 *Cities of God*, 108.

22 Ibid., 108-111. With the typical interpretation still collectively accepted by modern historians Thompson defines Ezzelino da Romano as "a tyrant." However, as we have seen in the essay on Canonization, Ezzelino is a complex case.

who hear it, for they are rendered worse by hearing and neglecting the word than by remaining ignorant.[23]

Newman argued that demonic phenomena had a double theological purpose of confirming the sanctity of the person who was capable to cast them away from the obsessed person while at the same time strengthening the teaching of the Church with their eloquent literacy of Scriptures.[24] Thus the Church was in daring need of demons as much as of saints.

In the twelfth century, at a point of crisis in the historical battle between the Church and secular society, lay communities attracted women particularly among lower classes of workers and artisans, but they also came from all walks of life: widows, orphaned women or women abandoned as children, abused and battered women, socially rejected, with serious illness or physical malformations and/or without possibility of marriage, and occasionally women from nobility or from prominent, local families. Female participation in these communities was a sign of destabilization of the ordinary female condition in society. For women the possibility for social stability was limited: there was either a good marriage or a monastic life, in order to avoid prostitution. Entering a monastery, however, required the support of a wealthy family willing to pay a considerable sum of money. A widow was considered nonproductive and was not welcomed back in the family unless she accepted a new marriage thirty days after her husband's death.[25] These associations of laywomen, as previously mentioned later on called *beghine, pinzocchere* or *mantellate,* became a new social outlet, a solution for marginalized women who, in the new dynamic of Italian communes, could not be part of the traditional female environment. Often they traveled from one community to another not having a stable situation that would allow them to settle in a fixed place. The new laywomen's communities at ease with city life recruited the daughters from aristocratic or powerful local families that traditionally would help a new establishment with their donations; but they were especially attracting women at the margin of society, searching for a safe space in the city and trying to find purpose in their social environment living together and supporting each other with work activity. These groups of women brought together by the same need of economical and social stability were a healthy natural outcome that allowed many women otherwise refused by society to survive; most of them were far from being "holy women."

With the increased power of a centralized Roman Curia, female communities, subject to growing criticism and at risk of being ostracized, acquired a re-

---

23 Barbara Newman, "Possessed by the Spirit: Devout Women, Demoniacs, and the Apostolic Life in the Thirteenth Century." *Speculum,* 73. No3 (July 1998): 733-770, 756.

24 Ibid., 749.

25 Meersseman, 280.

ligious identity in order to satisfy the Church's expectation. Sanctity and mysticism became commonly accepted events, part of the women's daily effort for survival. At the inception of this social phenomenon it is not clear, as Vauchez and Meersseman pointed out, that the grouping of laywomen could have a clear religious commitment. It would seem that being able to work together in a shared activity, to develop a certain type of business such as weaving, manufacturing clothing, artifacts, growing and selling vegetables and other products or having a role of service as midwives or nurses, was already a good motivation for these kinds of organizations. Soon enough, however, given the natural suspicion toward women's activities, we will find the Church pushing for a religious structure to be respected by the laywomen's communities. With the progressive stiffening of papal rules from 1215 to 1311, especially toward the end of the thirteenth century, religious obligation became stricter as also the suspicion was mounting and many communities were accused of heresy. Heretical movements were certainly infiltrating the same space in which the Church operated: otherwise, the frenetic inquisitorial activity steadily growing in the thirteenth century would not be explainable. It never has been openly recognized that heresy occupied a large space crisscrossing every aspect of Italian society. There is no in-depth study that shows how many Catholic devotional practices that developed at the time were in fact a reaction meant to counteract heretical beliefs: a few examples are the extreme popularization of the Eucharist and of the suffering of Christ on the Cross, the Cross as a universal symbol of penance, the emphasis on the stigmata, the issue of chastity in marriage; also, the focus on demonic possession was in the same category.[26] These were all points of contrast, for example, with the Cathars' belief system, which spread during the twelfth and thirteenth centuries from France to Italy and represented a real danger that undermined Catholicism. Catholics, then, needed to demonstrate the truth of their beliefs by the extraordinary intensity of practices meant to counteract the Cathars' doctrine. Preachers and inquisitors were hard at work and the faithful followers of the Roman Church were eager to gain Paradise with their penance.

There is denial among Catholic scholars who refuse to admit the pervasive influence of heresy in European society at a much deeper level than it was suspected. Vauchez, commenting upon the vow of chastity of Delphine of Puimichel and Elzéar, reluctantly observed:

---

[26] Barbara Newman in "Possessed by the Spirit": "It is surely no coincidence that the demons, according to their clerical scribes, became eloquent witnesses to sound doctrine at precisely the time that Cathar dualism flourished - with Jacques de Vitry and Thomas of Cantimpré among its most vigorous foes. For if demoniacs themselves reinforced the doctrinal and pastoral teachings of the church, especially those most controverted by the heretics, how could the listening public fail to recognize that the devil was no autonomous agent, as the Cathars maintained, but a subaltern firmly subjected to the will of God and the truth proclaimed by his Priests?" 749-750.

It would be speculative to speak of possible Cathar influence. To be sure, as René Nelli has shown, chastity, defined as abstaining from sexual activity, was considered by Catharism in Languedoc to be the highest form of love, because an unconsummated marriage did not result in procreation.[27]

And in the note giving reference to René Nelli Vauchez went on to explain:

> Let us not forget that for the Cathars procreation meant putting a damned creature into the world, and procreation was evil because it repeats the satanic operation of the incarnation of spirit in matter.[28]

In contrast with the Cathars' belief the Church gave more emphasis to the sanctity of marriage and consequent procreation.

The proliferation of lay communities influenced with their presence the religious space normally reserved to traditional monastic life and allowed for a freer approach to devotion and individual penance. Even though the main motivation for the formation of the lay women's associations was of socio-economic nature, soon enough women were forced to establish a more rigid religious structure to their community in order to avoid clerical negative reactions. On the other hand it seems that women adjusted easily to the necessity dictated by their situation because, ironically, laywomen's communities became active centers of saints' production, highly needed for the protection of every single city. As already noted, there were not many choices for medieval women: either an early marriage with dozens of children to bear, a life of prostitution or a monastic life. Being a holy woman was not so bad after all, particularly for wealthy women whose families could pay for their comfortable life in a rich convent. Lay communities offered the same opportunity to all women in a more democratic way: they were closer to Francis' ideal than any other institution. In any case, the opportunity of becoming a saint was not something to be refused, and many women asserted their talents and exalted their egos reaching success and appreciation in their society with the most daring ascetic exercises. Many were called saints and became patrons of the cities where they lived, others supposedly were possessed by devils and gave formidable spectacle to crowds of excited believers; some are still honored and volumes are written on them as they seem to have had extraordinary experiences.

MARGHERITA DA CORTONA: A TRUE SAINT?

One of the greatest examples is Margherita da Cortona, a strong-willed woman, who found the way to assert her individuality in a world that would not

---

27 *The Laity in the Middle Ages*, 196.

28 Ibid., 310 n. 20. The Cathars' doctrine is a subject far beyond the scope of this paper; however it is healthy to point out that an objective analysis of Catharism in Italian religious studies is largely overdue.

otherwise allow her to succeed in any other acceptable enterprise. Sanctity was her business and she went at it with vengeance as many other women did in need of appreciation. One characteristic of her saintly behavior was fasting, a hallmark of ascetic practices common to medieval religiosity. The most famous women saints fasted to the excess, starving themselves to death. Rudolph Bell is correct when he states in his work *Holy Anorexia:*[29]

> The fourteenth-century saint, like the twentieth-century patient says she cannot eat and denies that she is asserting her will or being stubborn. But it is her will that is at stake, and unless something works to deflect the contest, its logical outcome is death.

Medieval *holy women* wanted to have control over their bodies, to have a voice in their family that abusively made decisions for them and in society that marginalized them. In the impossibility of gaining control over their lives they were taken by an extreme desire to sublimate the basic instinct of survival, to be in total control of their bodies, following a religious teaching with which preachers saturated every corner of their cities. Preachers divulged a doctrine of hope for an*other life* on a different dimension, as spiritual beings outside the dreadful reality of a carnal body. Women followed the path toward the unknown and denied the reality of their bodies to bargain for a better world. It is quite understandable that when the body is in a state of shock for excessive food privation, visions and paranormal episodes may be the result. People believed in a supernatural world then as many believe in it now; there is much that we do not know yet about our potential and a healthy skepticism is in good company with an open mind. Margherita exhibited hysterical behavior that was not much in tune with true sanctity; but that perhaps did not matter, because the spectacular events she staged were great entertainment for the local public and certainly could not be repressed without creating discontent. Saintly women and men participated, willingly or not, to the intrigues of religious and civic authorities that used their fame and popular success to their political advantage. There was trouble, however, when the saint's *odore di santità* would suddenly change in smell of heresy in which case the Inquisition would be fast at work. In some cases, when the saint was already very popular with the public at large, it would have been unwise to call him or her a heretic. It is not hard to believe that in such a case the Church would swiftly cover up the heretical suspicion with good expedients. The building of a great basilica, an eloquent *Vita*, a papal bull, sophisticated philosophical interpretations and a few miracles could certainly be effective in building the figure of a saint if deemed necessary for the Church's image.

Margherita da Cortona is a great example of how a holy laywoman could be made to influence not only the local civil rivalry and the population at large,

---

29 Rudolph Bell, *Holy Anorexia* (Chicago and London: University of Chicago Press, 1985), 28.

but also Church politics at the highest level. The devotion for Margherita spanned from the small area of Cortona to the entirety of Catholic Italy. She became a beacon of renewed spirituality at a crucial time in Church history.[30] Her fame started locally in Cortona with the help and protection of the *ghibellini* Casali family, who were struggling to gain power. With the favor of the Casali family, Margherita acquired the role of patron to protect the interests of Cortona's people against the nearby city of Arezzo and its Episcopal seat that claimed to have the right over Cortona's jurisdiction. Essential to the procedure of becoming a holy patron was to have a good hagiographer capable of writing an inspiring *Vita*. The hagiographer was usually interested in projecting a powerful image of a saint destined to some useful function for the Church's political agenda. The *Legenda de vita et miraculis* was completed in 1308 by the Friar Giunta Bevegnati, Margherita's confessor from 1288 to 1290 and was approved by Cardinal Napoleone Orsini. In Giunta's work Margherita becomes in fact *filia Jerusalem...tertia lux in ordine ... Francisci.* [31] As Schlager affirms, Friar Giunta was "eager to promote the Franciscan penitential movement, the forerunner of the Franciscan Third Order."[32] Margherita's sanctity represented something larger than Cortona's local politics; it embraced the higher idealism of Franciscan spirituality represented by Francis and Claire, the first and second brilliant stars at the service of the Church. Margherita was then the third star, *tertia lux* in the *tertius ordo*, representative of the Franciscan Third Order and more popular than the official patron of the Third Order, Elizabeth Queen of Hungary. The hagiographer did not stop there: on a different spin that Margherita's life-tribulations justified, Giunta exalted the quality of penance she endured in order to purify herself from having been a sinner; thus the parallel with Mary Magdalena, the sinner par excellence, and with all *religiosae mulieres* who could not claim virginal purity before dedicating themselves to spiritual life. Margherita, *filia Jerusalem* was also a *nova Magdalena*, in remembrance of the woman who was the closest to Christ, closer than his apostles. The Virgin Mary must have looked somewhat intimidating with her immaculate virginity while the figure of Magdalena was very popular at the time especially among married women who could feel frustrated for a lost virginity and would then find respite in the success story of Mary Magdalena.

From the limited space of local Cortona Margherita's fame covered a much larger area that included Israel and the coveted city of Jerusalem. After the complete failure of the Crusades the Church was picking up broken pieces moving back the center of Christianity from the dreamed Jerusalem to Rome, with the symbolic event of the 1300 Jubilee, and defining the belief in a trans-

---

30 Anna Benvenuti Papi, *Castro Poenitentiae* "Cristomimesi al femminile," 141-168.

31 Ibid., 144. Trans.: *daughter of Jerusalem ....the third light of ...Franciscan Order*.

32 Bernard Schlager, "Foundresses of the Franciscan Life" *Viator* 29 (1988): 141-166.

formation of the Church itself as a new Israel. Margherita, new Magdalena and daughter of Jerusalem, symbolized the spiritual crusade she endured against her sins and the sublimation of her suffering to sanctity in parallel with the collective suffering of Christianity during the fight against the infidels and the Roman See's new position as a center of the Catholic Church. The intersection of multiple meanings in the sanctification of Margherita and the profound symbolism that fused her own personal struggle with the Church's universal renovation demonstrate the extreme complexity with which politics, religion, self-assertion and an extraordinary will to succeed conflated to give birth to a saint. Certainly there is no equal in our history to the Church's ability to renovate itself using at any cost the most unorthodox method. In a lucid analysis Papi explained the meaningful identification of Margherita with Magdalena. Margherita was a new Magdalena who moved at ease within the Franciscan Order; the Franciscan Order perfected the representation of its founder Francis in the vest of *alter Christus* and determined the coordinates of a seraphic *terra santa* in which to stage Margherita's feats. In Cortona, the New Jerusalem, a new Magdalena was following (or was made to follow) on the new Christ's footsteps. The renovation of a connection between the Western world and the less reachable sacred places in Palestine was happening as a crowning achievement of a complex translation. The Church, far from having been exhausted by the mechanic of searching for relics, wanted to propose those sacred places or even those figures that by now the infidel was making unavailable to Christianity. According to Papi in the identification of the real *terra santa* to the European Western world, one of the most significant transpositions is precisely the figure of Mary Magdalena, who arrived in southern France at the time of the apostolic Diaspora and was significantly rediscovered during the crusades. Magdalena came to symbolize the ideal of the conversion and the penitential pilgrimage to the holy land that preachers propagandized during crusades; except that then, having renounced the crusade, the ideal was modified in the inner-pilgrimage for all Christians who, in their own homes, could adopt the same crusader spirit and fight individual demons following the spiritual path of penance.[33] This is indeed a breathtaking image full to the excess of signifiers for what Margherita da Cortona represented as a *nova Magdalena*.

But from which origin and life experience did Margherita come to be crowned as the third luminous star in the Franciscan sky and identified with one of the most powerful women in Christianity? Or who was the real woman under the vestige of a saint? She was born in a modest family in central Italy, in present-day Castiglione del Lago. Rudolph Bell recounted her story in a down-to-earth way that is quite refreshing after having read so many extraordinary tales. At first she seemed to be a strong-willed adolescent with great

---
33 Papi, 146-147.

ambition and passion for life. She was in love with a young nobleman, Arsenio da Montepulciano, whose family refused to approve of their marriage because of her inferior social status. However, she accepted Arsenio's invitation to live with him at his residence. She was sixteen when she left home and went to live with Arsenio until when, nine years later, Arsenio was killed and, having had a child in the meantime, she was left alone with her son. As an unmarried woman with child, both her family and her lover's family rejected her. She was quite beautiful and still very young so that at that point she had two choices, either become a prostitute or join a religious community. Opting for religion, she arrived in Cortona with her son and she was fortunate to meet noblewomen who helped her to decide her next step: the Mascari's family gave her refuge and she became active with other women in charitable work or helping as a midwife. Donna Marinaria Mascari took her to the near Franciscan convent where she asked to vest as tertiary penitent but she was refused. Apparently the friars mistrusted her for being too young and also exceedingly attractive, but perhaps also because she was showing inappropriate behavior perceived by friars as not in tune with a penitent life. Later on it will be evident that Margherita did not have a great relationship with Franciscans because she moved from near the Franciscan convent to a new location above the city of Cortona in a cell attached to the church of Saint Basilio, and she also chose a new secular cleric as her confessor, Ser Badia. In any case Margherita was determined to go all the way on the path of sanctity. Bell wrote that she stated to her noble friends: "There will come time when you will call me saint, because saint I will be and you will come to visit me with pilgrim's staff and mendicant sacks hanging from your shoulders." Was this premonition or sheer arrogance? Bell commented:

> It was not only a negative amending for sins past but also a positive drive for outstanding holiness (here innocently confessed by Margaret in a way so frankly heterodox that it is surprising that her biographer in his enthusiasm let it slip through) that carried this woman to the destruction of her body. [34]

In fact it can be interpreted that for Margherita the determination to become a saint was really the determination to be famous and revered. She was looking not for humility but for control through fasting and hard-core penance. She demanded more attention and admiration than what she had experienced during those precious nine years of happiness in the rich home of Arsenio. These are speculative guesses, but so are the learned writings claiming Margherita's holiness. Margherita succeeded in her endeavor and was renowned for what people took for humility. Bell wrote:

---
34   Rudolph Bell, *Holy Anorexia*, 95.

> [...] Margaret became renowned for the exceptional humility with which she shouted out publicly her sins, moving her listeners to weep as she also discovered their defects and suffered with them for their misdeeds. Among her audience of penitents were not only humble people but also priests and even a visiting inquisitor.[35]

This must have been real theatre in the square of Cortona, perhaps on the church's steps in perfect harmony with the traditional spectacle of sacred representation. People were excited to call her saint and we still do the same to this day.

According to the *Legenda*, the penitential discipline practiced by Margherita was too extreme even for some of the Franciscans who were in favor of asceticism. But she felt she had to increase her fasting to demonstrate her spirituality and to counteract the suspicion of many who disapproved. Again, this was proof of her will. Her continuous dialogue with Christ was a dialogue with herself in which she found strength and motivation for persevering on the path of suffering. She was determined to destroy her body to the very end of herself: "I want to die of starvation to satiate the poor," she told her confessor.[36] It is then that the devil Lucifer joined the sacred theatre: as reported, the devil seemed to have given her some common sense advice inviting her to be moderate in her penance while the Christ would push her to follow harsh penitence as she wished. Practically the Christ figure represented her own will reinforced by the practice of fasting, and she might have had a better chance of salvation by following the devil's advice. Lucifer and his acolytes began to torment her, appearing to her in monstrous visions, but the Christ was ready to console her suggesting that she should not listen to anyone pushing her to act differently from what she wished.[37] Despite her great popularity many were not convinced of Margherita's sincerity, and that was probably an incentive for her to double up her fasting to a breaking point for her body. In fact, she killed herself by starvation.

It happened also to many other women under the illusion of holiness, such as Umiliana dei Cerchi, Angela da Foligno or Caterina da Siena, all very interesting figures of women who were desperately trying to find space for themselves in a chaotic environment. Among the people who were critical or suspicious of excessive penitence was the writer Francesco da Barberino, who in *Reggimento e costumi di donna* (1318-20), a treatise dedicated to women, comments upon the laywomen who dedicate themselves to religious life. He admitted that it was happening for different reasons: some women were too poor and wished to have an honorable life despite their poverty, others might have some secret illness that did not allow them to be married, others still had

---

35 Ibid., 96.
36 Ibid., 102.
37 Ibid., 380-381.

fear of hell; there were very few who acted exclusively for love of God.[38] Papi argued that Francesco da Barberino would have promptly accepted Lucifer's sensible argument to dissuade Margherita da Cortona from her spiritual pretention of sanctity. Like Francesco there were probably many others convinced of the insanity of aberrant devotion, but Friar Giunta was determined to give birth to a real saint and the Church was eager to see the result and collect the benefit from the magisterial transformation of Margherita in *filia Jerusalem* and *nova Magdalena*. At the end of her days, consumed by her passion and at the limit of her physical strength, she was still repeatedly tempted by her demon that in the shape of a serpent distracted her from prayer. Before dying she had the opportunity to attend to the final combat between her angel protector and the devil.[39] It is not clear to us which one could have been the outcome. Her death was announced to the people of Cortona as *un transito glorioso*, a glorious transit to the other world.

Holy women like Margherita da Cortona with such a great talent to serve the Church's politics, and be served by it, were not a common happening after all. There were many more women, hundreds of them, who had the merit to be the real protagonists of the extraordinary women's movement that, if carefully nurtured, could have brought splendid fruits. Medieval space changed dramatically in relation to these new associations, but women's communities were never allowed to have a positive development just as Francis' ideal failed to be recognized. The Franciscans, after the excitement for reform that Francis inspired, instead of following the pattern he indicated that could have immensely helped the women's associations, were never able to give breathing space to them. Franciscans went back to the traditional scheme of convent life, recruiting rich women among nobility or the well-to-do families of the emergent middle-class. Often the religious authority ordered them to take care of remaining laywomen's organization; already at the beginning of the fourteenth century, however, we have seen that in 1311 Pope Clement V declared that all beguines were heretics and laywomen's communities slowly disappeared, absorbed by regular monasteries. The beguines then became nuns in the enclosed area of a traditional monastery. The large medieval space rich in ferment and possibility, in which the laywomen's communities could have become a valuable social outlet for women's independence, became ineffective. Early in the thirteenth century, the excessive focus on extreme penitence alternated with episodes of laxity and corruption, which gave the first blow to those communities. Afterward the accusations of witchcraft and heresy, used by the Church every time it had to deal with some uncomfortable reality, definitely shrank the remaining available space to nothing. A two-hundred-year story ends here; the

---

38 Ibid., 208-212.
39 Papi, 39.

laywomen of old disappeared, although some nuns in the most ancient convents such as Santa Lucia in Foligno or Santa Maria di Monteluce in Perugia still today are called *beghine.*

CHAPTER FOUR

Sacrum Commercium

Finding the Real Francis

There is no other text in Franciscan literature like the *Sacrum Commercium*. It is the only document giving the unmistakable impression of a real Francis, whose light shines through the theatrical scenes involving the reader in the very essence of his life. He appears simply as a brother among his other brothers, neither as a blessed father nor as a saint.

Does the *Sacrum Commercium* solve the Franciscan Question? Certainly not. If the *Sacrum Commercium* might sound a true story for many, to a majority it remains an allegory, practically a fiction, merely representing Francis' spiritual aspiration toward an impossible ideal. To some, however, not even Francis' writings can give the same clear image of Francis' revolutionary solution to the ills of his time as expressed in the *Sacrum Commercium*. The ambiguity concerning the interpretation of documents, coming to us after centuries-old manipulation, is staggering: Francis' own writings, as precious as they are, appear merely like bit and pieces of gold hidden in a sea of historical mud.

One of the main problems in the interpretation of the *Sacrum Commercium*, as for the majority of ancient manuscripts, is the difficulty of understanding who produced the text and when. There is an ongoing discussion about the date of the *Sacrum Commercium*. As specified in the introduction of the *Sacrum Commercium*, in *Francis of Assisi; The Saint, Early Documents*,[1] we have seven manuscripts dated 1227 and another six not dated, thus raising

---
1 Volume I, p. 523. (St. Bonaventure, NY: New City Press) 1999.

the possibility of a different period. There is no compelling reason, however, to discard the date written on the seven manuscripts. Stefano Brufani examined all the found manuscripts; he discounted the date of 1227 and left the question open. Michael Cusato was more inclined to consider a later date in the context of the growing tension between Francis' followers and the official Franciscan Order after Gregory IX's bull *Quo elongati* (1230). Among a variety of different opinions, David Flood's interpretation made perfect sense. He accepted the date 1227, because he saw a direct correlation between the *Sacrum Commercium* and all the events happening before Francis' death. Tension was already building up against a too rigorous interpretation of the Rule and the discussion in the *Sacrum Commercium* revealed the kind of living debate among the brothers during Francis' time. It is important to consider how Francis appears in the *Sacrum Commercium* and Flood explained: "Francis acts within the brotherhood. The action in the *Sacrum Commercium*, however symbolic, belongs to the history of those years culminating in the stand-off at the general chapter of 1230."[2] In the *Sacrum Commercium* Francis, brother among brothers, was precisely how he was and wanted to be during his life: he was a man in search of truth. This is a very strong impression running through the scenes of the *Sacred Commercium*. It presents Francis in his youth together with his brothers searching for a new way, a revolutionary one that would change the balance in his contemporary corrupt and greedy society. It describes the real history of Francis and his brothers' struggle for acceptance in Assisi's thirteenth-century society driven by the frenzy of the new economy, commerce and material possession. Already toward the end of Francis' life the struggle was not with society at large, but within the brotherhood itself. Many so called brothers were in fact no brothers at all. Lady Poverty says: "Then there arose among us some who were not of our company, certain children of Belial, speaking vanity doing wicked things. They called themselves poor when they were not...."[3] Francis' intention was betrayed when he was still alive and aware of the many brothers who rejected his vision and fell back in the illusion of a material world.

The situation changed even more drastically after his death; Francis would never have wanted his own canonization and the clamorous building of a basilica in his name. According to Flood, in the *Sacrum Commercium* we contemplate real history, though under symbolic cover: "That is, the story in *Sacrum Commercium* possesses an analogical relationship to history."[4] Flood's observation concerning the difference between allegory and symbolism sounded

---

2   David Flood, *Poverty's Condition, a Reading of the Sacrum Commercium*. Haversack, Occasional Paper 2, 6.

3   *Francis of Assisi, "Sacrum Commercium,"* 38.

4   Flood, 7.

true. Many historians considered the *Sacrum Commercium* an allegory expressing a spiritual path toward perfection and discounted its importance as historical document. For Flood, instead, the text was a symbol that interpreted and represented Franciscan history from the very beginning of Francis' commitment to Poverty from 1209 to 1227 when, right after Francis' death, the rift between the brothers was already irresolvable:

> [...]We have two frames of reference, symbolical and historical [...]. SC is a symbol rather than an allegory because, primarily, it interprets early Franciscan history while representing it. [...] It traces the origins of those debates under which the brotherhood labored in 1227.[5]

Looking closely to the historical context, poverty, as Francis intended it, was too harsh and socially not acceptable. The lure of the commercial revolution was pushing people to accumulate coins and material possessions. The temptation was too great: *paupertas* was not attractive enough for those brothers who were fascinated by the novelty and purity of the Franciscan Order and wished to follow it, but could not practically adapt to the harshness of Francis' *forma vitae,* in particular to Francis' expectation of unconditional love for *paupertas*. It is necessary to note that the concept of *paupertas* did not refer exclusively to material poverty, as it was later interpreted, but to a life in common, in communion, with the most disadvantaged, the *minores*. The choice of living among the *minores* in society was the basic guiding concept of Francis' social reformation. It is precisely from *minoritas* that *paupertas* derived. The commitment to poverty did not mean that friars could not have everything needed for their existence. They provided to their basic material needs with their daily work in total equality with the poorest in their local community. It must then be clear that *paupertas* was strictly connected with the concept of *minoritas*. In Francis' *forma vitae* every individual would exercise his/her own talent for the well-being of all.

For the brothers who were not willing to accept Francis' program the Pope was ready to make it easier so that he could send friars in great number all over the world preaching and converting to Catholicism. Responding to the friars' growing concern for the interpretation of Francis' *Testament*, at the general chapter of 1230, Gregory IX presented the bull *Quo elongati* with which he made drastic changes in Francis' conception of *forma vitae*. Being a jurist Gregory transformed the *Testament* into a legal document with its own juridical life independent of its author. He claimed to know Francis' intentions; having been Francis' adviser, however, and the Cardinal Protector of the Franciscan Order, did not make his claim true. The bull that the Pope issued forced a change of dimension upon the Franciscan Order. Francis existed on

---
5   Ibid., 7-8.

a subtler plan that a majority of his followers did not share or perceive, much less the Pope who was most concerned with the practical world of material possession and power. If during his lifetime Francis' charisma could irradiate and guide few of his companions toward an extraordinary change in the quality of life, at his death the ordinary forces of greed and power took charge. The issue of poverty was originally strictly connected to the necessity of work. In the involution of Francis' *forma vitae* the word itself, work, disappeared from friars' daily lives, and in its place preaching became more pressing. Preachers, however, lived in the cities and were evermore learned and capable of sophisticated debates. At this point the real Franciscan spirit died. The original *forma vitae* slowly disappeared from the friars' lives: once meant to transform dysfunctional communities into self-sufficient, alive social cells, it remained an empty shell at the service of papacy. It testified to the historical misunderstanding of Francis' inspiring vision. The Pope declared that the brothers were not bound by the *Testament* and gave new guidelines to answer the most compelling issues.

Having considered briefly the historical background, we realize that *Quo elongati*, 28 September 1230, was only the first step toward a complete betrayal of Francis' *forma vitae,* but we cannot deduce from it that the *Sacrum Commercium* had to be written after its promulgation. In fact, *Quo elongati* was also the culmination of years of debate and tension within the brotherhood. In 1227 there must have been plenty of brothers aware of the different direction and meaning given by the Pope to Francis' lifelong struggle. The *Sacrum Commercium* was conceived while an intricate situation was evolving: it was already brewing during Francis' lifetime and certainly provoked a negative reaction among his closest and most faithful followers.[6] Right after Francis' death one or more of them might have decided to give a veiled account of their experience.

We do not know who the author was. This is not surprising, because at the time there was no compelling need to declare authorship as there is today; also, the author might not have desired to be recognized for fear of retaliation by brothers who thought differently. Without question it must have been someone very close to Francis, an insider who faithfully followed Francis in his daily itinerary and understood deeply his concerns. But does it matter who the author is? Trying to recognize a possible authorship seems, so far, to be quite hopeless: we have only educated guesses limited to considering well-known personalities belonging to Francis' circle. Could it be Caesar of Speyer? Perhaps, but he was not the only possible candidate. We do not know

---

6   *Assisi Compilation*, 18, 44. The events at the Chapter of Mats show already a fracture between the Pope and Francis in 1221. Also, during his illness Francis appears upset for the direction taken by people who "have snatched out of my hands my religion and that of my brothers."

all of Francis' followers at the time and there were thousands of them. A great majority remains unknown.

After Francis's death the Church exercised her power to appropriate and exploit Francis' movement transforming it in a useful tool. Gregory IX demonstrated Church politics at its best in his dealing with the Franciscan Order, even transforming the poor brothers into the worst kind of inquisitors, "hammer of heretics." Even though the Church created a scenario appositely devised to take advantage of Francis' popularity, Francis did not represent the official Church: it is quite clear in the *Sacrum Commercium* that Francis did not belong exclusively to the Roman Church as the Pope wished: he belonged to the world.[7] In the twelfth century and at the beginning of the thirteenth century there was no real distinction between different approaches to the interpretation of scripture. The author then could be among the non-orthodox Christians: there were many who were mingling with Catholics and in good faith called themselves Christians. There was no clear boundary between true or false believers. The definition of heretics, among whom were the Cathars, came later when the Church felt threatened by religious credos that challenged her power. Many Cathars, the *perfetti*, were highly educated and in tune with Francis' philosophy of life. There are some references in the text giving space to the possibility that the author might have been one of those Christians rejected by the Mother Church. Lady Poverty recounts the creation of man and original sin stressing passages in the scriptures that are typically emphasized in Cathars' doctrine. For example, she says: "After the garment of innocence had been stripped away, the Lord made him a garment of skin, signifying with it his mortality."[8] In his study on Catharism, Jean Duvernoy, described a meeting of *perfetti* in Arques, Aude, in 1300, in which the *perfetto* Jacques Authié, explaining the Creation of man, referred to the same passage, though with a different twist because the entity that gave the garment of skin was not the Lord but the Devil.[9] Lady Poverty also mentions that nowhere she found peace until the Christ himself came to earth: this declaration reminds the reader of the Cathars' mistrust for the Old Testament. Lady Poverty laments: "From that time I found no place to rest my foot, while Abraham, Isaac, Jacob and the others just ones, received as a promise riches and a land flowing with milk and honey. In all these I sought rest and found none […][10] " Moreover, Lady Poverty expresses her disappointment at Costantine the Great's false peace, responsible for having encouraged and made possible the growth of Church's material power: "Unfortunately, a short time later peace was made and that

---

7   SC, 63.
8   SC, 29.
9   Jean Duvernoy, *La Religion des Cathares, Le Catharisme*. (Bibliothèque Historique Privat, 1989), 62.
10 SC, 30.

peace was worst than any war. [...] My bitterness is now certainly most bitter during a peace in which everyone flees from me, drives me away, does not need me, and abandons me."[11] This was a point of contention held by Cathars against the Roman Church, because Constantine's gift to Pope Sylvester I in the year 315 initiated the Catholic Church's material dominion in western Europe.[12]

If many might be repelled at the idea that the author could be a Cathar, perhaps we can consider other possibilities: why not a woman? Certainly there were learned laywomen, enthusiastic followers of Francis. Certainly during Francis' life women were part of the brotherhood and their life was more flexible and free compared to later times. Historically, discrimination against women started when the Church became suspicious of women's influence upon men's religious congregations: before that, women were practically free to move in their society and practice their religion. If this is even more repellent than the previous one, could we conceive perhaps a cooperation of two or more disciples who were eager to let the world know the true story? Considering that nothing is sure in Francis' life, scholars have a choice of various scenarios according to their own bias and belief systems. By now Francis' historical reality seems to be shrouded forever, but perhaps there is still much to discover at least in the realm of possibilities.

The story in the *Sacrum Commercium* is simple. Francis is at the beginning of his peregrination and together with his companions wished to find Lady Poverty who had the key to the paradise on earth. It then becomes clear that the entire work is an exaltation of the glory of *paupertas*. It brings the reader through the Order's history, its commencement and decline. Francis' symbolic ascent with the friars from Assisi to the mountain, where they finally found Lady Poverty, culminated in the central *Grand Discourse* with which Poverty recounted her origin and story explaining how her embracing poverty ended with failure in most religious communities. The failure was due to infiltration of negative elements within the community:

> In the end, however, there arose among us some who were not of our company, certain children of Belial, speaking vanities, doing wicked things. They called themselves poor when they were not: and they spurned and maligned me whom the glorious men about whom I have already spoken loved with their whole heart. They followed the path of Balaam of Bosor, who loved the reward of wickedness; men corrupt in mind, deprived of truth, supposing their quest to be one of piety. They were men who took up the habit of holy religion, but did not put on the new man and only covered over the old.[13]

---

11 SC, 34.

12 The Donation of Constantine, in 315, was proved to be a fraud by the fifteenth-century humanist scholars Nicola Cusano and Lorenzo Valla, who wrote *De falso credita et ementita Constatini donatione declamatio?*

13 SC, 38.

The three rivals who contrasted poverty were Greed, "the immoderate desire to acquire and retain riches," Discretion that "would be better called confusion" and Foresight or "the destructive forgetfulness of all good."[14] These were the vices causing the degeneration of the Order. Highly symbolic was the descent from the mountain: this time Francis and the friars were in the company of Lady Poverty. They rested at their place where they had a meal with Lady Poverty. At the end of the meal after a peaceful rest the Lady asked to see their cloister: "Taking her to a certain hill they showed her all the world they could see, and said 'This, Lady, is our enclosure.'"[15] Here again we find something in common with heretic's belief: the brothers have a much larger purpose than the one willed by the Roman church. Their direction is the entire world; they are not limited to the physical structure of any church.

Michael Cusato interpreted this passage as Francis' explicit rejection of the newly dedicated Basilica in Assisi, because, at this point, the friars and the Lady would be turning their back to the basilica looking, instead, in the opposite direction out of the city to the countryside. While for the Pope Gregory IX the basilica in Assisi represented the symbol of the new Franciscan Order destined to a glorious future at the service of the Church, for the companions it represented the betrayal of *forma vitae*, thus the total misunderstanding of the important place of poverty held in the life of *fratres minores*. As the story goes, at the end the brothers did not return to the city, which meant a complete rupture with their society. There is a clear impossibility of integrating the brotherhood's original ideal with the ordinary way of life among a society of greed and selfishness. The market economy, spouse of material greed, impeded the healthy development of a new generation of true Franciscans. Who can find something different today?

---

14 SC, 39.
15 SC, 63.

CHAPTER FIVE

FRANCISCAN WOMEN

THE MONASTERY OF SANTA LUCIA IN FOLIGNO
AND THE *LEGENDA* OF SANTA CHIARA.
FROM BEGUINE COMMUNITY TO *SCRIPTORIUM*

During the fifteenth century female convents flourished in north-central Italy revealing a flurry of extraordinary literary production together with an unprecedented intellectual activity among women: the monastery of St. Lucia in Foligno is particularly interesting for being emblematic of this new direction among female institutions.[1]

The monastery originated with a group of women coming from Sulmona in 1424. In his *Umbria Serafica* Agostino da Stroncone gives news of their arrival.[2] The women escaped incidents of violence in Sulmona between religious and civil authority. They were all from the same noble family of Sulmona and found support in Foligno's local noble family, the Trinci. Their names are recorded as Gemma and her daughters Margarita and Chiara, accompanied by a relative, Lisa, and under the direction of Alexandrina, Gemma's cousin. Alexandrina seemed to be the more enterprising and soon became abbess of Santa Lucia. The official date for the arrival of the exiled women is 22 July

---

1 A version of this essay appeared in *The Cord*, Volume 60 No 2 (St. Bonaventure: New York, April - June 2010): 118-137, and in *MIR International Journal of Business and Social Research*. No 1 (December 2011): 57-69.

2 Between 1670 and 1680 Father Agostino Mattielli da Stroncone gathered all available information on Franciscan movement in Umbria since the beginning in 1208. The original manuscript of his work, *Umbria Serafica* is in the Archive at the *Portiuncola* in Santa Maria degli Angeli. Luciano Canonici. *Santa Lucia di Foligno. Storia di un monastero e di un ideale*. (Edizioni Portiuncola: S.Maria degli Angeli, 1974): 14, n5.

1424 or according to other sources, perhaps 1425.[3] Their intention was the foundation of a monastery to complement an earlier older establishment; there was in fact in the same location a group of unidentified women living in a kind of beguine community under the Augustinian rule. All the women in Santa Lucia, the new and the old ones, were determined to remain completely on their own, which is without any assistance from friars as was usual for a female community. This did not seem to be the friars' fault: the women refused to be under friars' surveillance unless they could have as spiritual directors the friars of the *Osservanza* presided over by Friar Paoluccio Trinci, who had just founded the convent of San Bartolomeo of Marano. In 1427, under the Rule proclaimed by Urban IV, all the women at Saint Lucia received direction from the Friars of Saint Bartolomeo of Marano, as they wished.[4]

Santa Lucia is an example of the evolution from the loose organization of the first laywomen's communities to the rather different structure of a monastery directly ordered by papal authority. Like the other famous convent of Santa Maria di Monteluce in Perugia, between 1450 and 1580 St. Lucia in Foligno became a *scriptorium* of educated nuns, a place where women, usually wealthy and of noble origin, would take residence while pursuing literary activity. This represented a historical development often preceded by the formation of communities of laywomen.

From Lay Community to Regular Convent[5]

It is necessary to clarify the social background that determined the evolution from lay community to regular convent and also to examine the reasons that provoked the decision of many women to enter a religious community. Already in the previous twelfth and thirteenth centuries, a great number of women chose to separate themselves from their family joining other women with a common purpose. Considering the complexity of that time's social environment it would be unrealistic to assume that women flocked to the convent's life purely for religious vocation. The socioeconomic structure existing in the fifteenth century was the consequence of previous historical happenings that caused and pushed for the formation of enclosed areas exclusively dedicated to women: there was no free space for women in medieval society. Already in earlier time the Church's direction was evident: soon the feminine gender would be the most controlled species on earth.

In the twelfth and thirteenth centuries, a particular reaction to a rigid social environment caused a unique phenomenon that spread all over Europe, tak-

---

3   Ibid., 33-35.
4   Ibid., 41-43.
5   This chapter develops the subject of women's conditions already approached above in chapter three.

ing multiform shapes according to local customs: many laywomen gathered together sharing their living space and organizing their daily lives in communities. Were all the women participating in a common life dedicated to religious pursuit? Or were there other important elements more or equally compelling that pushed them to search for support sharing their life and activity with others?

Laywomen formed at first small groups loosely organized, but soon they attracted an ever-greater number of women particularly from the working class, but also from the rich middle class, from the merchant class and from nobility. As Father Meersseman explains, one of the main reasons for the multiplication of non-enclosed women penitents was the monastery's economic structure. He argues that many of these women attracted by the lay-pietism current at the time, coinciding with the beginning of Gregorian reform, did not possess an adequate dowry for entering a regular traditional monastery.[6] This was not the only problem. In fact women from all walks of life were attracted by the new opportunity of living together. There were all kinds of them, and they all found themselves in need of shelter and protection. Lay communities sprouting everywhere became the answer. Economy and sociopolitics were important, often prevalent aspects of the social dynamic. Social issues, local politics and religious practices were completely intermixed, thus constantly influencing each other. Despite the effort to separate and distinguish civil administration and Church administration, it was in practice not possible to avoid the Church's influence upon civic affairs. Thompson argues that in the late thirteenth century, in its effort to compete with the Church, the civic jurisdiction modeled itself on religious structures claiming legal legitimacy over Episcopal authority, but too often did not succeed or it did at the cost of bloody conflicts.[7]

The women exiled from Sulmona were precisely victims of the type of situation described by Thompson. In their city the conflict between the local powerful families reached the internal life of the convent where they resided, the Monastery of Santa Chiara founded in 1268-1269 by Floresenda di Palena daughter of Tommaso, Lord of Palena, near Chieti. Noble families in the region were all deeply involved in the convent's maintenance where their female relatives lived in a very comfortable and rich environment: political struggle among them affected the women's lives in the convent because they also took

---

[6] Gilles Gerard Meersseman, *Ordo Fraternitatis, Confraternite e pietà dei laici nel medioevo*. (Herder Editrice: Roma, 1977): 282.

[7] "The growing division of civil and ecclesiastic jurisdictions paradoxically led the commune to cultivate an ever more sacred ethos for itself. [...] Secularized communes needed their own divine legitimacy. They sought it in heaven, invoking the protection of new patron saints and on earth, saturating their laws, assemblies, and communal institutions with sacred rhetoric, symbolism, and ritual." Augustine Thompson. *Cities of God. The Religion of Italian Communes 1125-1325*. (Pennsylvania: Penn State University Press, 2005):108.

sides for their family. One of these conflicts more serious than others between the families of Merlini and Quadrari of Sulmona was the cause for the escape of the women who found refuge in Foligno: they saved their lives using the social structure appositely created for women's protection.

In the fifteenth century the lay communities of old with their social flexibility were disappearing and the available social structure for women was then the monastery or convent organized as a strictly religious establishment. Women were forced to establish in their community a rigid religious program, guided by a growing deep mistrust toward the feminine gender. Twelfth- and thirteenth-century lay communities were a good solution and offered the same opportunity to all women in need: as we already said, they were indeed closer to Francis' ideal than any other institution. Nonetheless, women's communities, under increased suspicion by Episcopal authority, were never allowed to have a positive development, just as Francis' ideal failed to be recognized. The Franciscans, after the great excitement for reform inspired by Francis, instead of following the pattern indicated by him that could have also helped greatly the women's associations, were never able to give breathing space to them. Franciscans went back to the traditional scheme of convent life recruiting rich women among nobility or the well-to-do families of the emergent middle-class. Often the friars were ordered by religious authority to take care of the remaining laywomen's organizations; however, already at the beginning of the fourteenth century in 1311 Pope Clement V declared that all beguines were heretics and laywomen communities slowly disappeared absorbed by regular monasteries. This corresponds to the evolution of Santa Lucia in Foligno from beguine community to regular convent. The beguines were transformed into nuns in the enclosed area of a traditional monastery and a different story took place, the story of the many convents in north central Italy that were heirs of the laywomen communities, but completely reorganized according to papal jurisdiction. Some nuns in the most ancient convents such as Santa Lucia in Foligno or Santa Maria di Monteluce in Perugia still today remind scholars of the old beguines.[8]

THE SPECIFIC CASE OF SANTA LUCIA IN FOLIGNO

In the convent of Santa Lucia in Foligno, two women among others exemplify the kind of female activity characteristic of the fifteenth-century monasteries: Sister Caterina Guarnieri of Osimo and Battista Malatesta of Montefeltro, who changed her name to Sister Hyeronima. We know of their existence thanks to the chronicle of the monastery, whose main author has been Caterina Guarnieri.

---

8   Jacques Dalarun and Fabio Zinelli refer to the previous establishment upon which the convent of St. Lucia was organized as a « sorte de beguinage » some kind of beguine community. «Le manuscrit des sœurs de Santa Lucia de Foligno, I. Notice». *Studi medievali*, 46 (2005): 117-167.

The chronicle of the monastery is contained in a manuscript now located in the Archive of the *Curia Generale, Ordine dei Frati Minori* in Rome, codex A 23, dated at the beginning of the sixteenth century. The existence of this codex was announced by Giovanni Boccali at the International Convention, *Clara claris praeclara*, 20-22 November 2003 in *S.Maria degli Angeli, Assisi*.[9] From the handwriting it is evident that only one person wrote the manuscript. It is not in good condition, thus reading it is somewhat difficult. Sister Caterina Guarnieri was in charge of the chronicle at the Monastery of Santa Lucia and was the first copyist to document the events at the monastery from 1425 to 1536. She is the daughter of Stefano Guarnieri of Osimo, chancellor of Perugia in 1466-1488. We know from her father's testament in 1484 that Caterina Guarnieri was the twelfth child among five brothers and eight sisters.[10] She died in 1547. The chronicle continues by the hand of Sister Antonia, the scribe who worked as a copyist after Caterina's death. Sister Antonia also writes the eulogy for Caterina: "Caterina was a good woman both for family inheritance and for her virtue; she is remembered for her saintly life and had an important position at the convent. She was abbess for three years and wrote numerous works for her sisters whom she loved greatly."[11] Caterina does not seem to have been more than a copyist;[12] however, without doubt she contributed with excellence to the intellectual ferment of the new humanistic culture that was developing in parallel with a more organized monastic life. Looking at her family situation it can be argued that entering the convent might have not been her personal choice. She had eight sisters: how many of them were able to have a convenient marriage particularly after their father's death? With the escalating discrimination against lay communities, the only decent alternative to marriage was the regular convent, and it was indeed the best solution in a woman's destiny. It is then possible that an intellectually gifted woman would prefer entering the convent where she had the chance to exercise her talent as in no other place available to the female gender: university was an exclusively male territory. Religiosity was part of the deal: being a pervasive force in society, religion was automatically drawn into daily life without necessarily meaning

---

9   Giovanni Boccali, "Leggenda in rima su S.Chiara d'Assisi." *Frate Francesco*, 71(2005): 389-414.

10   Her father's Testament is in U. Nicolini. "Stefano Guarnieri da Osimo, cancelliere di Perugia dal 1466 al 1488." *L'Umanesimo Umbro, Atti del IX Convegno di Studi Umbri* (Gubbio, 1974): 324-329.

11   Paraphrased from the Saint Lucia Chronicle's eulogy written by Sister Antonia: "L'ultimo di' de marzo (1547) morì la matre sora Caterina da Ozimo, donna da bene de sangue e de virtù, e veramente d'essee hauta a memoria per le sue virtù e sancta vita...Epsa matre scripse el libro de Melchiade e quello de Hierusalem, e io sora Antonia, ci la adiutai ; e multe altre cose à scripte per consolatione de le sore, ad le quale epsa matre portava grandissima carità e amore. Fo vicaria nove anni e tre anni fo abbatissa, poi Dio la menò alla gloria beata a remunerarla de le sue buone opere [...]" Giovanni Boccali. "Legenda in rima su S.Chiara d'Assisi nel cod.A23 dell'Archivio della Curia generale dei Frati Minori in Roma." *Frate Francesco*, 71 (2005):389-414, 390.

12   J. Dalarun and F. Zinelli "Poésie et théologie à Santa Lucia de Foligno. Sur une *laude* de Battista de Montefeltro", *Caterina Vigri. La santa e la città*. (Atti del Convegno Bologna, 13-15 Nov. 2002):19-43.

or implying a deep belief in everything was preached by the Church. We do not have a record for what happened to the whole Guarnieri family, but we know that out of nine girls three became nuns: Caterina entered Santa Lucia in Foligno in 1489, Gerolama, Caterina's older sister, joined the nuns at St. Maria di Monteluce in Perugia and so did Susanna, the younger sister, right after the father's death in 1494. To believe that they entered the convent exclusively for religious vocation would be a narrow, partial view of the women's actual position in Italian fifteenth-century society. Taking into account the growing control upon women's communities as well as the rampant authority in the hand of the Inquisition, at any time ready for accusation of heresy, the idea that the activity at Saint Lucia, as in any other convent flourishing in Italy, could have as its main inspiration a "profound spiritual need" (profonde exigence spirituelle)[13] sounds quite unrealistic. By the same token the beautiful description of the nuns' lives given by Mario Sensi is colored by poetic imagination more than by historical reality. As Sensi rightly observes, for absence of documentation we know nothing of the internal convent life, but immediately after this statement he goes on describing the nuns' inner experiences: "characterized by hard penance, mysticism and by Franciscan peace. [...] Submitted to their spiritual directors these religious women searched only for a silent asceticism and a life of poverty. [...]Their ideal was to follow on the way indicated by Saint Chiara. [...]"[14] Certainly the description paints the image of what the Church wished and still today wishes to be, not necessarily of what really was.

The general direction in fifteenth-century Italian society was to create more monasteries, thus avoiding the awkward situation in which a woman would find herself without a man. A demonstration of this trend is in a later document written by a notary from Bologna around 1550. The notary Giovanni Boccaferro addressed a *Discorso sopra il governo delle monache* (*Discourse on the discipline for nuns*) to the bishop of Bologna, Giovanni Campeggi, in order to take position against an ecclesiastic reformation that had the tendency to eliminate the economic and social reasons for the existence of monasteries. Boccaferro argues that this would be dangerous for the social stability and explains the absolute necessity of feminine convent life for various reasons strictly connected to demographic, social and economic problems. He affirms convincingly that monasteries are the "only remedy for women who cannot be married." This was an opinion shared by the majority of citizens.

---

13 Jacques Dalarun and Fabio Zinelli. « Le manuscrit des sœurs de Santa Lucia de Foligno, I. Notice». *Studi medievali*, 46.(2005) : 117-167 +VII fig., 27.

14 Mario Sensi explains: «Anche per la scarsità della documentazione, è stata invece finora poco studiata la loro vita interna, caratterizzata da aspre penitenze, da slanci mistici e soprattutto da una francescana serenoità.[...]Docili alla guida dei loro direttori spirituali queste religiose altro non cercavano che l'ascesi riservata e pauperistica. Loro ideale fu quello di ripercorrere la strada di Chiara d'Assisi [...] » citation in Jacques Dalarun and Fabio Zinelli «Le manuscrit des sœurs de Santa Lucia de Foligno, I. Notice». *Studi medievali*, 46. (117-167 +VII fig..): 147.

Boccaferro's strong conviction represents the apex of a long process already evident during the fifteenth century manifested in the increased importance and growing number of feminine convents connected to the Franciscan movement of the *Osservanza*.[15] It was also a confirmation of the usefulness of the previous beguine movement that had first recognized and found a solution for women's social need: the old beguine community was now transformed and institutionalized in conformity with an imposed religious structure becoming ever stricter as time brought increasing challenge to the Church's authority. The earlier beguine establishments were mostly composed of women trying to fight an unkind social reality, sharing their work, mostly labor, in order to survive. A laywomen community had a more democratic goal compared to the fifteenth-century's monastery populated with high frequency by wealthy and well-educated women. Their motivation in entering the convent might have been similar to the beguines' need for a community, because they also found themselves at a loss in their society. The difference though consisted in having the support of their powerful families: their wealth allowed for more freedom and communication with the exterior world. As a consequence they had the opportunity to use their good education at the service of the community, as Caterina Guarnieri did recording the events at the monastery, or they could be dedicated to learning and creative literary activity as Battista Malatesta of Montefeltro did, following the particular interest of the time, which coincided with the new cultural movement of humanism.

MONASTIC SCHOLARSHIP

In Santa Lucia in Foligno Battista Malatesta of Montefeltro distinguished herself among the most learned for knowledge and creativity. She was mentioned and praised for her many talents by Sister Caterina in her *Ricordanze*, the chronicle of St. Lucia's Monastery. Battista was born in 1384 and married Galeazzo Malatesta, lord of Pesaro, in 1406. She entered Santa Lucia in 1444 or 1445 with the name of Sister Hyeronima and was followed by her daughter Elisabetta already married to Pier Gentile Varano, Lord of Camerino. Elisabetta had lost her husband in one of the many local wars and brought to the convent also her daughter Costanza Varano. In a typical situation Battista Malatesta, a wealthy sixty-three year old lady with a good marriage behind her and whose family inheritance could afford to pay for her new residence, used the convent as a place for a protected retirement. Her husband Galeazzo Malatesta was still alive but probably too busy being at war as most noble men

---
15 « [...]essi monasterii debbono esser il ridotto di quelle che maritar non puonsi » Gabriella Zarri. «Monasteri femminili e città.» *Storia d'Italia. La chiesa e il potere politico.* Annali v. 9 (Torino : Einaudi Editore, 1986): 359-429, 361-363.

of the time.[16] Her daughter Elisabetta, whose social position was affected by her recent widowhood, accompanied her. Hyeronima's granddaughter Costanza followed as well, probably too young to make her own decision, but in a difficult social situation having just lost her father. Clearly the convent represented a safe haven for women who did not have men's protection: contrary to the old beguines, however, they needed to be wealthy in order to pay for their security. Battista Malatesta found refuge at Santa Lucia together with her two female relatives and stayed until her death in 1448. As customary, she left a testament in favor of the monastery.

Hyeronima was very learned in humanistic culture; she wrote Latin orations and Italian poems, leaving at her death letters and poetry in Latin and Italian, some still unedited. She must have done most of her work before entering the convent because her life did not last long afterwards. Caterina Osimo never met her because she joined the convent in 1488 while Hyeronima died in 1448, but certainly her fame was still alive among the other sisters from whom Caterina could gather information for her chronicle. According to Caterina, Hyeronima "era docta in ogni scientia liberale et maxime in strologia, et havea grande cervello di componere et rimare laude...." ("She was learned in every liberal science especially in astrology, and she had great ability for composing rhymed *laude*...."). Coming from the noble family of the counts of Montefeltro and destined to a marriage with Malatesta, another noble and very powerful family, Hyeronima lived in a privileged situation, open to the possibility of developing her intellectual interest. Leonardo Bruni Aretino, a well-known humanist scholar, who, in a long letter in Latin, qualified her as "a very learned woman," also praised her remarkable creative talent.[17] Bruni wrote his letter between 1423 and 1426, before Battista entered the convent; he advised the lady to read classical Latin authors. He was obviously concerned that she should learn what is most proper for a woman; thus, for example, she should give priority to religious literature and moral writings while she would not need to practice the rhetorical art of speaking in public that, just as the art of war, was not destined to women. As Jacques Dalarun comments we do not know whether Battista followed all of Bruni's advices.[18] But certainly in her letters she did practice public discourse and participated in the political life of her time; she also excelled in astrology, which, as other sciences, Bruni did not consider necessary for women. Besides her communication with Bruni,

---

16 According to other sources Galeazzo Malatesta was already dead when Battista entered the convent. Luciano Canonici. *Santa Lucia di Foligno. Storia di un monastero e di un ideale.* (Edizioni Portiuncola : S.Maria degli Angeli, 1974): 64.

17 Giovanni Boccali, "Leggenda in rima su S.Chiara d'Assisi." *Frate Francesco*, 71(2005): 389-414, 399.

18 J. Dalarun and F. Zinelli. "Poésie et théologie à Santa Lucia de Foligno. Sur une laude de Battista de Montefeltro" *Caterina Vigri. La santa e la città. Atti del Convegno Bologna* (13-15 Nov. 2002):19-43, 29-32.

Battista had an intellectual relationship with her father-in-law, Malatesta I Senatore of Pesaro, a learned man with whom Battista exchanged poems and correspondence.

In the manuscript under consideration, codex A 23 in Rome, only one poem has a clearly stated authorship attributed to Hyeronima Battista. The title is: *Laude devota delli dolori mentali del Signiore, composta da Madonna Hyeronima da Pesaro, sora del Monastero de Sancta Lucia de Fuligni*. This *laude* has been amply studied and commented on by Dalarun and Zinelli. Another *laude* dedicated to Santa Chiara of Assisi, also in the same manuscript, does not have a clear attribution. At the beginning of the manuscript Caterina acknowledges the author of Chiara's *Legenda: una sora del monastero de Sancta Lucia*, (a sister at the monastery of Saint Lucia). She does not specify the name, but Giovanni Boccali attributed without hesitation the *Legenda* to Sister Hyeronima. Unfortunately, we can never or rarely be sure of a manuscript's original author; in fact, Jacques Dalarun noticed incongruence in the manuscript and cast doubt on the attribution to Hyeronima. Dalarun argues that in the manuscript located in the Archive of the *Curia Generale, Ordine dei Frati Minori* in Rome, only one *laude*, the one just mentioned, is clearly of Battista. The situation is complicated by the fact that the manuscript contains writings from other authors such as Bonaventura and Caterina Vigri. The two *laude*, the one clearly attributed to Battista and the *Legenda* of Santa Chiara are not together in the manuscript and actually they seem to belong to two different pamphlets later on tied up in the same codex. According to Dalarun the only good argument for attributing the *Legenda* to Battista is in another codex, the manuscript of Pesaro, in which, however, only a part of the *Legenda* is said to belong to Battista.[19] Dalarun is in the process of clarifying the *Legenda*'s authorship.

The *Legenda* is an invocation and a prayer in Old Italian, with the description of few traits of Chiara's life: it consists of 62 octaves and one quatrain. Caterina Guarnieri introduces the laude: *Incomenza la legenda della gloriosa sancta Chiara composta in rima da una sora del Monasterio de Sancta Lucia de Fulignj* (Here starts the story of the glorious Saint Chiara composed in rhyme by a sister at the Monastery of Saint Lucia in Foligno). The most prevalent theme in the poem is the theme of *light* with much wordplay with the name *Chiara* (Clare): the Italian proper name *Chiara* is also a feminine adjective and means *light* corresponding to the English adjective *clear;* instead the English noun *light* translates in Italian as *luce* or *lume*. The Italian *chiarissima luce* is a *very clear light*. In a significant parallel the major characteristic in Dante's *Cantica* of *Paradiso* is precisely the light that pervades the paradisiacal environment and becomes ever more resplendent and clear as Dante as-

---

19 Pesaro, Biblioteca Oliveriana, 454, II (XVII - XVIII centuries), ff.44r-45v.

cends to experience divine glory. God is supernatural Light. With the most extraordinary talent Dante infuses light in every word that describes his Paradise: thus, the reader also receives light and a sense of Dante's divine inspiration. For an Italian reader the perception of light in Dante's Paradise is indeed the most salient experience that distinguishes this *Cantica* from the other two, *Inferno* and *Purgatorio*: this is a quality of Dante's poetic genius that is almost completely lost even in the best English translation. The author of the *Legenda* seems to be aware and sensitive to Dante's expression of light, and we find in her poem the same effort for composing words as clusters of light whenever she describes Clare's divine illumination. The many words associated with the theme of light are without doubt a mannerism inspired by Dante's superior poetic strength. The striking resemblances to Dante's style are from both the *Commedia* and the *Vita Nova*: in one of the octaves (number 8) the poetess convincingly paraphrases Dante's verses in the *Vita Nova* (I, XXI) illustrating the noble demeanor of Beatrice appearing as supreme love among ordinary men: the same is applied to the image of Clare.

There are other *topoi,* popular in Franciscan hagiography that the nun is using, such as the comparison of Clare to a plant grown out of Francis's spirituality—a plant *(pianta)* giving a *fragrant flower (aulente fiore)*— the mention of Clare's virginity, obligatory requirement for sanctity, and her mother's prophecy that she will give birth to an extraordinary holy woman. Also in octave 51 there is a reference to *I Fioretti* with which the writer reports words taken by Francis' preaching on the square of Montefeltro, Battista's birthplace.[20] This might be a small element in favor of Battista's authorship. However, the poetic imitation of Dante is most important because it reinforces the idea and demonstrates the fact that the author was a woman extremely well learned and with an unusual literary knowledge.

As highlighted in the following octaves the words she is using in order to impress images of light in the reader's mind are the following: *splendore* (splendor, brilliance, brightness), *chiaro splendore* (clear splendor, brilliance), *splendida* (magnificent, splendid), *splendente, scintillante/scintillando* (shining), *stella* (star), *lucido splendore* (shiny splendor), *luce splendida e serena* (splendid and serene light), *(il)luminato* (enlightened), *divinamente viva rosa* (divinely alive or vivid rose), *gloriosa luce chiara* (glorious bright light). She repeats them in different and new combinations practically saturating the whole poem; but more than every single word the pervasive style of the poem lights up the spirit. In the same way Dante opens the door of Paradise and shows to the perceptive reader a glimpse of divine light.

---

20 Caroli Ernesto, "Biografie di San Francesco. I Fioretti; Considerazioni sulle Stimmate" *Fonti Francescane.* (Padova: Editrici Francescane, 2004): 1234. Boccali gives reference to it in "Leggenda in rima su S.Chiara d'Assisi." *Frate Francesco,* 71(2005): 389-414, 400.

1. Jo prego quella **vergene pura et bella**
   Che è matre del mio creatore
   Che doni gratia alla mia mente fella
   Ch'io possa dir de quello **aulente fiore**
   Et parlar possa io de quella **stella**
   Che a tucto el mondo venduto ha **splendore**
   Ciô è ch'io possa dir de quella **pianta**
   Che tenne vita evangelicha sancta.

2. Et questa fo la **sposa del Signiore**
   Che **sancta Chiara** per nome è chiamata
   Et fo de **vita** si **chiaro splendore**
   Che molta gente per le' s'è salvata
   Et tanto piacque al suo redenptore
   Che in cielo et in terra l'à glorificata
   Tucta s'alegra la corte **divina**
   Della sua **luce splendida et serena**

1. I pray that **pure and beautiful Virgin**
   who is mother of my creator
   so she might grace my feeble mind
   so I could sing of that **fragrant flower**
   and speak of that **star**
   who gave **splendor** to the whole world
   that is I could say of that **plant**
   having had an evangelical santly life

2. This has been our **Lord's lady**
   called with the name of **Saint Clare**
   and she had **a life** of such **a clear brilliance**
   that many people through her were saved
   and so much she was liked by her Redeemer
   in the sky and on the earth he glorified her
   The whole **divine** court rejoices
   for her **splendid and serene light**

***

4. Jnanze che nascesse **el nobil fiore**
   Alla sua matre fo da Dio mostrato
   como seria **si lucido splendore**
   che tucto el mondo ne seria luminato
   et quando ebbe inteso tal tenore
   fo tucto el suo cor lectificato
   tornô a casa alegra con gran festa
   et parturl la matre benedecta

4. Before the **noble flower** was born
   to her mother by God was shown
   she would be such **a shiny brightness**
   the entire world would be enlightened
   and when she had understood the news
   her heart had been full of happiness
   she went home with joy and celebration
   and gave birth the blessed mother

***

6. Questa **splendente stella in Asese**
   Nacque de stirpe degna et generosa
   jn puerile età mostrô palese
   esser **divinamente** *viva rosa*
   onde mirabil cosa
   pareva a chi sua vita contemplava
   et ben considerava
   Sempre habitare Dio nella sua mente

6. This **shiny star** in Assisi
   was born from noble and generous descent
   already as a child demonstrated
   of being a **divinely vivid rose**
   thus a wonderful thing
   seemed to whoever admired her life
   and regarded
   how always God lived in her mind

***

> In forma dunque di **candida rosa**
> mi si mostrava la milizia santa
> che nel suo sangue Cristo fece **sposa**;
>
> Le facce tutte avean di **fiamma viva**
>
> **ché la luce divina** è penetrante
> per l'universo secondo ch'è degno,
> sì che nulla le puote essere ostante.
>
> O trina **luce** che 'n unica **stella**
> **scintillando** a lor vista, sì li appaga!
>
> Dante. *Paradiso* Canto XXXI v.1-29

8. Et ben che como tesoro nascoso
Jnfra la gente non se demostrava
pure come piacque al suo dolce sposo
ogni omo la sua vita laudava
et era lo suo nome si chiaroso
che resplendeva dove non andava
siché ogni gente de lei diceva
Como figliola divina pareva.

8. And although like a hidden treasure
among people she did not show herself
as it was agreable to her sweet Lord
every man would praise her life
and her name was so bright
that would shine wherever she was going
for every person would say of her
that she looked like a divine girl

> Negli occhi porta la mia donna Amore,
> per che **si fa gentil ciò ch'ella mira**;
> ov'ella passa, ogn'om ver lei si gira,
> e cui saluta fa tremar lo core,
> **sì che, bassando il viso, tutto smore,
> e d'ogni suo difetto allor sospira**:
> fugge dinanzi a lei superbia ed ira.
>
> Dante *Vita Nova* I, XXI

30. Et poiché da Francesco fo adornata
Chiara *splendente luna fra* le stelle
Jn *verso a sole piglia sua tornata*
Acompagniata da quel fraticelli
Jn sancto Angiolo de Panzzo fo intrata
Dove **piantô li primi germoncelli**
Jncomenzzando II cum gran fervore
la vita sancta del nostro Segniore.

30. Because she was adorned by Francis
Clare shining moon among the stars
Toward the sun she goes
accompanied by the friars
in Saint Angelo of Panzo she entered
where she **planted the first tender shoots**
beginning with great fervor
the saintly life of our Lord

***

51. Fo questa **gloriosa *luce* chiara**
de **obbedientia** serva deputata
Al lei **verginità** fo sempre cara
et fu per lei **humilità** mostrata
De **strecta povertà** fo sempre avara
Et mai volse de lei esser privata
lei tre voti amô con tanto affecto
che ogni pena per lor parea dilecto.

51. **This glorious bright light**
committed servant of **obedience**
always loved **virginity**
and gave example of **humility**
never wanted to give up **poverty**
never wanted to be without it
she loved dearly the three vows
so much that any penance seemed a pleasure

> Francesco preaching at the castle of Montefeltro, birthplace
> of Hyeronima: *Tanto è bene quel ch'io aspetto, che ogni pena
> mi è diletto.*
>
> *I Fioretti – Considerazioni sulle stimmate, 1*

Tracing the process of the transformation of women's communities from the beguine movement to the fifteenth-century's regular convents it becomes evident that the old beguines left no history behind or perhaps just scattered information. In Italy, more than in other countries as in Flanders or France, they were mostly illiterate, very poor and probably too busy trying to survive to find respite in any intellectual activity. When the laywomen communities were restructured and increasingly controlled by the Church the environment changed dramatically: together with stricter religious rules, wealth and material well-being entered convent's life allowing for the leisure of literary creativity. Perhaps we will never know for sure to whom we owe the *Legenda* of Santa Chiara, but no matter who is the author the composition is an admirable example of feminine poetic inspiration from an age and a place, the convent, in which wealthy and noble women could afford to have a story to tell. If Battista Malatesta is the poetess, she shows in her verses cultural awareness of religious themes and at the same time she also reveals in depth literary knowledge that could have been foreign to other well-educated nuns but not particularly learned in literary production. Dalarun points out that Battista's work deals exclusively with religious subjects, but in contrast her poetry is completely in tune with contemporary literary courtly rhetoric: there is nothing in Battista's writing, or very little, resembling the primitive *laude* in Jacopone da Todi's style, which was still popular in the fifteenth century as shown in Caterina Vigri's poems.[21] This could be a point in favor for the attribution of the *Legenda* to Sister Hyeronima. The *Legenda* of Saint Chiara is a beautiful poem with a clear influence from Dante's style; just for this reason we would be inclined to prefer the attribution to Battista, considering her sophisticated knowledge of the famous influential poems of her time. However, there might be other more compelling factors for a different interpretation as argued by Jacques Dalarun.

The examples of poetry given here are just a taste of the learned activity exercised by women at the Monastery of Santa Lucia during the fifteenth century. Besides Caterina Guarnieri and Battista Malatesta there were others who contributed to the fame of the convent. In the nineteenth century Foligno's historian Faloci-Pulignani remembers the peculiarity of Santa Lucia, a real cultural center in which many women could practice their talent. From the monastery they could irradiate their knowledge and interests to many similar centers in other Italian cities such as Messina, L'Aquila, Bologna, Mantova, Ferrara, all taken by the intellectual ferment of the time. However, the convent of Monteluce in Perugia was indeed the closest in spirit to the sisters of Santa Lucia; an active exchange of ideas and literary production between their *scriptorium* guaranteed to both convents an important role in the development of humanistic culture. Feloci-Pulignani reminds us of the presence in

---

21 « Il est d'autant plus remarquable que sa production poétique traite exclusivement de matière sacrée [...]. Mais à l'inverse [...] la poétique mise en œuvre est résolument celle de la grande rhétorique courtoise. On ne trouve guère trace, dans ses œuvres, de la syntaxe et des figures de la laude primitive. Il y subsiste fort peu, par exemple, de la manière d'un Jacopone de Todi dont le succès est pourtant encore vif au XV siècle en particulier dans le milieu franciscains, comme en témoignent les laudes, plus archaïsantes de Caterina Vigri » J. Dalarun and F. Zinelli."Poésie et théologie à Santa Lucia de Foligno. Sur une laude de Battista de Montefeltro" *Caterina Vigri. La santa e la città. Atti del Convegno Bologna* (13-15 Nov. 2002):19-43, 32.

Santa Lucia of many well-educated, noble young girls from the best families of central Italy. Once in the monastery, besides daily prayers and manual work they continued to practice their love for literature. They sang poetry in Italian, Greek and Latin, wrote letters and chronicles, composed books, nourishing their knowledge with the study of classics and pursuing intellectual relations outside the convent with many learned men of their time.[22]

From the old beguines of lay communities to the enterprising wealthy nuns of later monasteries, women found their way through social discrimination. They were capable of surviving marginalization by using and reversing to their advantage the same religious establishment that was relentlessly persecuting them. Were they really religious, devoted women, committed to a profound spiritual life? Many more findings of documents, chronicles and manuscripts will probably continue to puzzle our minds creating new questions and challenging our present awareness of the ever-changing shape of history.

---

22 Luciano Canonici. *Santa Lucia di Foligno. Storia di un monastero e di un ideale.* (Edizioni Portiuncola: S. Maria degli Angeli, 1974): 85-86.

CHAPTER SIX

THE UNBEARABLE LIGHTNESS OF FRANCIS' *FORMA VITAE*[1]

HERMENEUTICAL ISSUES: THE FRANCIS OF HISTORY AND HAGIOGRAPHY

Francis' early vision and way of life developed in history with unforeseen consequences giving shape to the Franciscan Order. *Minoritas,* the choice of living among the *minores* in society, was the basic concept guiding Francis' belief; it was from *minoritas* that *paupertas* derived. It meant that the brothers would live in perfect harmony with the poorest and the less fortunate, exchanging the basic necessities for a healthy life, in which no one would have more than what s/he needed. Francis' Lady Poverty[2] was not threatening, imposing an existence of suffering and ascetical privation. As already stated, the commitment to material poverty did not mean that friars did not have everything needed for their existence. They would provide for their basic material needs with their daily work, begging only when necessary, in total equality with the poorest in their local community. *Paupertas,* then, was strictly connected

---

1 The title refers to the novel written in 1984 by Milan Kundera, *The Unbearable Lightness of Being.* By the same token Francis' *forma vitae* was a brief moment of beauty destined to disappear into history.

2 Lady Poverty, as we have seen in a previous chapter, is the protagonist of the *Sacrum Commercium,* a tale recounting Francis' desire to meet Lady Poverty. It narrates the final encounter with the Lady from whom he will never be separated. It is also the triumph of *fraternitas,* a quality of communal life organized upon the practice of a *commercio salutare* meant to allow for complete social equality. This was the hallmark of Francis' spiritual intent that was never implemented by the Franciscan Order. The *Sacrum Commercium* is considered an allegory hiding under its symbolism the truth about the regression of the Franciscan Order after Francis' death. The majority of scholars agree in dating the *Sacrum Commercium* after Gregory IX's bull *Quo Elongati* in 1230 as a reaction to the wrong direction taken by the Order.

with the concept of *minoritas,* as suggested by Michael Cusato in his lectures.[3] Also, the issue of poverty was originally strictly connected to the necessity for friars to have work, manual or otherwise according to individual talent. But in the evolution of Francis' *forma vitae,* throughout the thirteenth century, work disappeared from the friars' daily life when preaching became more urgent. The total disappearance of the work issue, so central to Francis' practice, reveals a complete detachment from Francis' *forma vitae* as stated in the *Early Rule.* The drastic transformation operated by Gregory IX in *Quo elongati* was only a first step toward an increasing manipulation of meanings leading to the deformation of the original Franciscan intent.

Among the various components of a complex social condition, considering the linguistic problems related to the interpretation of words, it is also necessary to keep in mind the minimal knowledge we have of Francis' everyday life, for which we have to rely on hagiographical tales, often received with various interpretations by modern historians. One aspect that has probably not helped the understanding of Francis' life and deeds is the strong bias in favor of a spiritual reading which was quickly proposed right after Francis' death in 1226 and still continues to this day.[4] The constant reference to Francis' sainthood, something Francis himself completely rejected, has clouded or given an unnecessary supernatural tone to Francis' pragmatic vision.

The passage from Francis' experience to the establishment of the official Franciscan Order [5] can be described as a jump from an existential dimension, immersed and in tune with a practical reality, to another ever more detached and alienated from social values. In this paper we follow the two contrary directions taken on one hand by both the official Franciscan Order and the Church's representatives and, on the other, by the brothers closer to Francis,

---

3   Michael Cusato, SFS 507, *Early Franciscan Movement,* fall 2008.

4   The romanticized interpretation of Francis as a highly spiritual figure is so common that by now it is taken for granted. Raoul Manselli, a well-known scholar, gives a spiritually inspired, romantic image of Francis. In the classic example of Francis repudiating his father's wealth he explains: "By despoiling himself of the garments in which so often he had sung, danced, played and shared with his friends in worldly distractions, Francis was repudiating his entire past ...displaying his penitential intentions. His penance... was taking the most rigorous form of the *sequela Christi...* it was the goal of following the example of Jesus in its ancient and severe tradition of *nudus nudum Christum sequi (being naked to follow the naked Christ)* the watchword coined in his time by St. Jerome." *St. Francis of Assisi,* (Chicago: Francis Herald Press, 1988), 59. Dominic Monti also recounts the same scene with a similar emphasis on Francis' "dramatic gesture." *Francis and his Brothers; a Popular History of the Franciscan Friars* (Cincinnati, Ohio: St Anthony Messenger Press, 2009), 13. A writer who exemplifies at best the interpretation in favor of a romanticized spiritual Francis, by now the prevalent popular image, is Valerie Martin in her *Salvation: Scenes from the Life of St. Francis* (New York: Knopf, 2001). Regretfully, this is indeed a most fantastic invention. Gilles Gerard Meersseman has a less dramatic and realistic view of the same episode. *Ordo Fraternitatis, Confraternite e pietà dei laici nel medioevo.* (Roma: Herder Editrice, 1977).

5   Pope Honorius III officially approved the Franciscan Order on November 29, 1223. Afterward the Franciscan Order went through changes that were sanctioned by Pope Gregory IX with *Quo Elongati* in 1230, moving the Order farther away from Francis' *forma vitae.*

the friars, later called Spirituals, who wanted to remain faithful to the original *forma vitae*, however already deformed through time. The extreme rationalization active among learned Franciscans, masters in theological debates, culminated in Peter of John Olivi's subtle theorization. Ironically, even though in principle Olivi wrote in defense of the original Franciscan spirit, the subtlety of his discourse on *usus pauper* undermined his goal because, by its very sophistication, it muddied the intrinsic purity and simplicity of Francis' *forma vitae*. Olivi's writing was used and misused by the Church and the Spirituals as well as by their lay followers.

For the purpose of this writing, we examine the work issue together with the evolution of the *usus pauper* debate. In fact the two issues cannot be separated without changing the nature of Francis' original intent. Apparently, considering the Catholic Church's struggle for political power, a negative outcome could not be helped. The Church facilitated, perhaps unwittingly, the triumph of all the intellectual, rational elements contrary to Francis' practical vision. This is still a plague in contemporary history among researchers in Franciscan study, oscillating between the allure of spirituality and the attraction for sophisticated reasoning, both enemies of Francis' *forma vitae*.

As already mentioned we need to account for the transformation of language through time so that often we cannot be sure we really completely understand the nature of facts as they are reported to us from existing documents. Also we consider the great mysterious space where social relations evolved in a way unbeknownst to us; events took place influencing the outcome of history that we will never completely understand. No one can establish for sure whether at the beginning there was a clear religious connotation attached to Francis' community. Was religiosity a necessary element that determined the existence of these communities or perhaps the religious dimension was added later to justify their presence in the eyes of the Church? Was Francis a spiritual being, as Gregory IX and later Bonaventure ventured to create, or did he decide to conform as far as possible to the Pope's desires in order to avoid persecution? There were certainly several impossibilities and some incongruence between Francis' *forma vitae* and the Church's expectations. The joy and lightness of Francis' experience was soon unbearable to many.

As reported in a previous chapter (*Saints and Demons in Medieval Space*), André Vauchez mentions Father G.G. Meersseman as a unique case of "intellectual probity as a historian" because, "debunking century-old myths," he did not hesitate to contradict common assumptions among scholars.[6] In fact Meersseman describes the extreme complexity of the medieval environment in which a variety of elements intersected and where religiosity, even though

---

6 André Vauchez, *The Laity in the Middle Ages. Religious Beliefs and Practices*. Ed. Daniel Bornstein, Trans. Margery Schneider (Notre Dame, IN, and London: University of Notre Dame Press, 1987), 108.

maintaining a central place, was only one of them. Certainly, the Church had a strong influence in all matters, material or spiritual, and its overriding concern was to counteract the Emperor's political influence impeding its expansion. The intricacy of the social structure with its mix of religious and economic ferments created a complex scenario not easy to decipher. We can say, following Meersseman, that the economic and political situation in Italy in the twelfth and thirteenth centuries did greatly affect people's attitudes toward religiosity, and it is very possible that economy and socio-politics could be the prevalent aspect of the social dynamic. Twelfth-century Italian society had manifest symptoms of internal crisis among the regular traditional religious orders and also between clerics and the laity. Considering the complexity of the social environment and the various problems inherent to the transformation of language, which in our time has lost the flexibility and polyvalent nature of the medieval discourse, Francis himself can be seen in different roles or imagined according to our modern interpretation that may not correspond at all with the historical reality of Francis' *forma vitae*.

Meersseman, for example, projects a Francis not so different from other hermits simply following a common trend that started between the second half of the eleventh and the first half of the twelfth centuries.[7] He has a down-to-earth manner of recounting the beginning of Francis' vocation, which is quite refreshing. He portrays an individual immersed in the regular atmosphere of his time, following attitudes dictated by the contemporary social problematic, doing in fact nothing extraordinary. The famous scene in which Francis gives up his clothes and stands naked in front of the bishop is related by Meersseman in very simple terms explaining the legal procedure required in order to obtain the Church's privileges.[8] Francis had left home and had given himself up as a worker at the church of S. Damiano. As a person working for a church, he had the right to be under the Church's jurisdiction and his father did not have legal power to force him back home. However, as the Church's representative explained to Francis and his family, Francis had to go through a legal procedure that is to publicly renounce his family's possessions and to change into a religious habit.[9] Francis promptly did just that. Since the very beginning, then, wanting to follow his wish for a simple life outside the rampant materialism of the mercantile era, Francis had to use the ecclesiastic structure typical of his time: not necessarily was he in harmony with Church politics or was he reli-

---

[7] Gilles Gerard Meersseman, *Ordo Fraternitatis, Confraternite e pietà dei laici nel medioevo*. (Roma: Herder Editrice, 1977), 246-247.

[8] Ibid., 356.

[9] Ibid. "L'episodio descritto dai biografi del santo come una scena teatrale, implicava invece una sottile questione giuridica che il giudice ecclesiastico formulò in questi termini : se Francesco vuol essere trattato come *donato e persona ecclesiastica*, con diritto al *privilegium fori*, deve rinunciare alla sua parte dei beni familiari e prendere l'abito religioso (*habitum mutare*)."

gious in accord with Church doctrine. Certainly, once responsible for the life of his followers he had to promise obedience, but who can say we have proof he was truly a submissive Catholic, as we like to believe today?

Let us also not forget that at the beginning of the Franciscan movement we are dealing with lay communities comprising men and women as it was already tried in other similar social groups. In any case it is important not to focus exclusively on Francis' brotherhood as if it were the most original and exclusive manifestation of extraordinary spirituality. What we often interpret as coming from divine inspiration was in fact a necessary reaction to the social ills of the time; mainly, the constant power struggle between Church and State deeply affected the life of all citizens, more so the men and women belonging to the inferior social classes not even classified as citizens in their own right. Francis tapped into an immense reservoir of human energy and talent ready to find a social outlet. There were other valuable experiments active at the time: religious groups perceived as dangerous were fought and finally placed under control by the Church.[10]

To Meersseman's description of Francis as a simple hermit not acting much differently from others, a common species at that time, we can contrast David Flood's more heroic Francis, who guided a conscious reaction against Assisi's corrupted system. Assisi's government promised peace to its citizens; but it was a false peace. Francis and his brothers "declared their intention to withdraw from the relationships and properties of Assisi. ... In chapter 7 of the basic document and in the chapters born of 7, they fixed the socio-economic basis of their life apart from Assisi's ways."[11] By working within Assisi's community while refusing to use money as exchange for their work, the brothers were initiating a completely new socio-economic relationship based upon real need. In this new system there was a place for every member of the community, rich and poor sharing their skills without allowing for an accumulation of money that would have created an imbalance. This interpretation of Francis' action focuses upon the originality of his *propositum vitae* consisting in a unique commitment in his relationship with the profit economy growing in the thirteenth century.

The creation and the development of financial institutions with the increasing use of coins or money had transformed the traditional environment of social exchange through barter and gifts. Very simply, Francis thoroughly rejected the new economy and advocated the organization of a different model based upon a sharing of goods and services while caring for each other's individual needs. The fulfillment of everybody's real need also meant real peace.

---

10   We refer to the numerous groups composed by penitents and beguines, male or female without specific directions or particular groups like the Umiliati or the Waldensians.

11   David Flood, "Peace in Assisi in the Thirteenth Century" *Franziskanische Studien*, 1 (1982), 68-80.

This was a bold statement, which sounds as unachievable today as it did in Francis' time, but it was perhaps perfectly possible if the Catholic Church could have found the strength to follow Francis in his vision. It did not.

Historians' perception of Francis' life and deeds oscillates between these two very different interpretations: the devout, sweet hermit living in evangelical poverty who experienced mystical ecstasy at the end of his days, or the lover of *minoritas,* socially involved in "transformative politics," working with his brothers to "marginalize Assisi."[12] A combination of both composes an extraordinarily saintly figure.

The socially involved Francis is to be favored, not because it is clearly the one closer to history, but because his figure fits today's particular need for social awareness manifested through the Franciscan desire to be of service: service to others is mandatory. It is clear that working without payment in money or accumulation of possessions would have transformed the socio-economic environment. It would have given an equal share to every individual, leveling all questions of ambition for power and prestige. Certainly, it would have been an ideal society, in which the concept of *paupertas,* the total refusal of money and possessions, was central. *Paupertas* did not mean exclusively material poverty: the result of working in *paupertas* should have been a careful balance in which each community member would have paid keen attention to the needs of others, sharing goods in complete equality with the poorest and less fortunate. Flood's Francis is a revolutionary figure very appealing to our modern taste for his clever pragmatism: while flying to meet the Lord he had his feet well on the ground.

Which one is closer to the truth? The hermit or the revolutionary? Francis' image coming to us through centuries of deforming evolution has bits and pieces of both. It is the image of a saintly figure in good harmony with animals more than with human beings and determined to honor Lady *Paupertas,* but not so keen on work. From the Giotto-like medieval paintings he looks at us like an ascetical man too intent on pursuing mystical rapture to have the slightest interest in social problems. If it were ever true, Francis' determination in fighting social ills was not successful at all: the Church or society at large did not favor social changes that could have played against their political power. It was preferred to keep the *status quo* and to give to the wider public the image of a sweet, peaceful sanctity still daily fed to the children of Italy and popular today.

But how much more interesting, fruitful and perhaps also closer to reality can be the perception of history when considered from drastically different points of view. As for historical truth, who knows? Readers choose the authors

---

12 David Flood, *Francis of Assisi and the Franciscan Movement* (Quezon City: The Franciscan Institute of Asia, 1989), 49.

who better respond to their own propensities. In accord with the mood of the time a talented author may or may not appeal to public interest. Sometimes, through the fluctuation of human sensibility, an author's work changes meaning and purpose in the eyes of the public, and critics then delight in new interpretations. It becomes clear how difficult it is simply to know where the truth is. In fact, when we discuss an author and try to interpret him or her, we really talk about ourselves. Certainly, truth comes in many shapes and colors, just as many as we do.

In the thirteenth century, Francis' *forma vitae* was soon to become a cause of bitter debate within the Franciscan Order, while his image lost its profound humanity since he was conveniently transformed into an angelic figure far away from earth and certainly not involved in any social transformation. After this first general impression of him, we will try now to make some sense reading the documents that more closely reflect Francis' original intention for his community. With the intention of understanding the relation between work and *paupertas* in Francis' *forma vitae,* we have to examine the texts available to us for a possible glimpse into what may have been Francis' experience.

Work in the *Forma Vitae*

The Early Rule, the *regula non bullata*, is the first document drafted by Francis and his companions in 1209, orally approved by Innocent III and put into final form around 1220 or 1221. The concise language describes a lifestyle characterized by the simplicity of a direct communication between brothers and sisters sharing the pain and the joy of creation. It has been extensively studied and commented upon. The most accepted view is David Flood's textual analysis that recognizes several layers added through time to the original. It testifies to the development of the brotherhood from its beginning to the drafting of the second Later Rule, the *regula bullata*, approved in writing by the Pope Honorius III in 1223.

Many people wished a return to the original purity of the first Christians, and there was a popular tendency to criticize the Church's materialism and corruption. Francis' originality probably consisted in his personal charisma and *joie de vivre* that won the hearts and minds of many who decided to follow his example. Today's basic understanding, as explained by Flood, is that the Rule developed at the same time, in concomitance with the change in the brothers' lifestyle: their *propositum vitae* initiated in 1208 was transformed into the *regula bullata* of 1223, terminating in Francis' *Testament,* a document judged to be non-binding by the papacy in 1230, not long after Francis' death.[13] In the text of the Early Rule as it has come down to us, I want to focus on par-

---
13 David Flood, *La nascita di un carisma* (Milano : Biblioteca Francescana Provinciale, 1976), 48.

ticular passages of chapter 7 that seem to translate Francis' original intention concerning the brothers' daily activities and their approach to money:

> Let the brothers who know how to work do so and exercise that trade they have learned, provided it is not contrary to the good of their souls and can be performed honestly [...] And for their work they can receive whatever is necessary except money. And when it is necessary, they may seek alms like other brothers. And it is lawful for them to have tools and instruments suitable for their trades [...]. Wherever the brothers may be, either in hermitages or other places let them be careful not to make any place their own or contend with anyone for it. Whoever comes to them, friend or foe, thief or robber, let him be received with kindness. [14]

This is a complete description of how brothers and sisters were supposed to occupy their days and behave with others, "friends or foes." It is clear that they could exercise a variety of activities, not necessarily just labor, according to their experience and social skills. The Latin text uses the word *ars* translated into *trade*: "*Et fratres qui sciunt laborare laborent et eamdem artem exerceant quam noverint [...]."*[15] In Medieval Latin *ars* is highly ambiguous with a variety of different meanings. It might refer to the skill or workmanship of an artist, to a craft, a profession, a theory but also to *scientia* or ability to learn, knowledge, creativity.[16] By using the word *ars* Francis leaves open a whole range of possible, completely acceptable, activities so that the brothers can participate at every level of their social environment. This important factor is lost in the translation in modern English: the word *trade* seems instead to refer to *exchange* or *commerce*, a more restrictive meaning. In the same way, the Latin verb *laborare* does not refer to the English *labor* or manual work: *laborare* is very close to the Italian *lavorare* which means simply *to work*, generically any type of work: manual, intellectual or other. We also notice the possible use of a figure of speech that may have been common in everyday language and is still used today: in Italian, the language closest to Latin, "to work with their hands" may refer to someone who "works without anyone helping him," giving then a different twist to a possible meaning.

In an article presented at a conference in Todi, 1980, on the subject of "Working in the Middle Ages," Antonio Ivan Pini suggests that there is a lack of research on the study of working activities and professions in medieval

---

14 *Francis of Assisi: Early Documents, The Saint.* Vol. I Edited by Regis J. Armstrong, J. A. Wayne Hellmann and William Short (New York: New City Press, 1999), 68-69.

15 Giovanni Boccali, *Textus Opusculorum S.Francisci et S.Clarae Assisensium* (Assisi: Ed. Portiuncula, 1976), 26.

16 In *Giotto and the Orators* (Oxford: the Clarendon Press, 1971), 9-15, Michael Baxandall explains the evolution of the language. He points out that in the passage from Latin to vernacular some terms, such as *ars*, were highly ambiguous and could be defined only by the context in which they were used: "The word *ars* (skill, craft, profession, theory, treatise) is an example.... *Ars* had been used in medieval Latin in most of its classical senses...."

Italy. He also affirms that the meaning of *ars* is generically "work" and indicates all kinds of professions, both organized in corporations or as individual ventures. He attempts a classification of the work activity in several Italian cities based upon the documents available in every specific location. In any case he confirms the versatility of the word *ars* that may refer to great varieties of occupations. [17]

It is hard to understand when and why the interpretation concerning the friars' activity was assumed to be *labor* or manual work, instead of *ars*. Manual work was associated with uneducated people of low social standing: being connected with a low social class, it was naturally despised by scholars, merchants, clergy, noble men and women and everyone for whom working with their hands was diminishing to their social position. It is still so, though in a lesser way, in European society. This transformation of meaning played a pivotal role in the constitution of the Franciscan Order and in our modern understanding of Franciscan history. It is notable that various commentaries on the Rule not long after Francis' demise mention only manual work; the idea of an organic community in which every member could express his talent in an activity useful to all was never really understood. Luigi Pellegrini mentions that "*Ars* has a precise semantic value at that time: different from *labor* and *servitium*, it indicates a particular work that requires specific competency."[18] The word *ars*, then, is a most essential detail: it is the key to a correct understanding of Francis' plan for his brotherhood.

Moreover, his expectation was that not only were the brothers supposed to practice their own talent, their natural gift, but also, no matter which their activity, they were not going to be paid with money. They would receive in exchange only what was necessary for their subsistence; in this way they could form an entirely independent and sustainable community. This was in obvious tension with the mercantile mentality rapidly developing in Francis' time. The success of Francis' *forma vitae* would have directed society toward a completely different outcome, but Francis' role was to plant only the seeds still waiting to be nurtured today. At the time of the Early Rule, when hopes were flying high in Francis' small group of brothers, there were already at work powerful negative forces among the brothers themselves who were responsible for bringing down Francis' community and depriving it of the original energy.

---

17 Antonio Ivan Pini, « Le arti in processione. Professioni, prestigio e potere nelle città-stato dell'Italia padana medievale » *Lavorare nel medioevo : rappresentazioni ed esempi dall'Italia dei secc. X-XVI*, 12-15 ottobre 1980 Convegni del centro di studi sulla spiritualità medievale (Università degli studi di Perugia XXI: Todi, 1983): 67-107 here at 74.

18 Luigi Pellegrini, « Fratres qui stant apud alios ad serviendum vel laborandum », *La grazia del lavoro*, Ed. Alvaro Cacciotti and Maria Melli (Milano: Biblioteca Francescana, 2010), 37-57 here at 43.

So far we have detected an important difference in quality already between the original Latin text and its translation in modern English. Now we will see that in the text of the 1223 Later Rule there is also evidence of a shift, backing away from the commitment to work claimed in the Early Rule. The text says in chapter five of the Later Rule:

> Those brothers to whom the Lord has given the grace of working may work faithfully and devotedly so that while avoiding idleness, the enemy of the soul, they do not extinguish the Spirit of holy prayer and devotion to which all temporal things must contribute. In payment for their work they may receive whatever is necessary for their bodily support of themselves and their brothers, except coin or money, and let them to do this humbly as is becoming for servants of God and followers of most holy poverty.[19]

There is no mention of any choice to "exercise that trade they have learned." This is much more ambiguous: does it mean that once they entered the community their work experience may not be valuable? What precisely will they be required to do as work? It is hinted that perhaps not all of them may have the grace of working; what, then, are they supposed to do? If the writers of the Later Rule wanted to clarify it, certainly they did not succeed: all is set up for confusion and misunderstanding. In any case, the purpose of working is "avoiding idleness;" it is not to create an economically sustainable environment that is not forced to rely on the material structure of the then current society. Francis mentioned the same purpose of avoiding idleness in the Early Rule as well; there it did not appear as the main purpose, but rather as a collateral consequence that was certainly to be desired. The shift is from Francis' pragmatic vision integrating a spiritual vision with the intelligent use of human potential to an abstract and spiritualized approach. In a few years, from 1209 to 1223, the original intention had already given way to the pressure of political interest and the consequent homogenization of religious communities sprouting all over the continent. Francis was one among many desiring to honor Mother Earth and its spirit creator; his charisma and special vision of life attracted crowds of enthusiastic followers and made him and his brothers particularly vulnerable to the Church's controlling power. His distaste for the use of money and the absolute prohibition to the brothers to base their activity on coin and money as the rest of society among which they were living was just too difficult for many of them. Was Francis' an impossible request? Why was it never even considered feasible, except perhaps by a few companions faithful to his vision at the very beginning of Francis' experiment? We do not really know. We do have, however, a superabundance of intellectual specula-

---
19 *Francis of Assisi, Early Documents*, I, 102-103.

tions, which study the cultural environment that allowed for the birth of several communities bent on a life of penitence.

Lester K. Little, for example, explains the parallel course of the new economy based on money, "the life blood of this new market economy"[20] and the history of spirituality in which "the approximate period 1000 to 1300 marks a high point in creativity and diversity."[21] In fact the proliferation of religious communities is astonishing. Little identifies a "line of reform" that since the very beginning is in tune with what will become Francis' search for *paupertas*. The emphasis was on a keen attention to the Gospel and on material poverty, the refusal to use money. This was a common attitude in numerous religious communities. Was it coming from fear of a foreign element, money, injected into a still traditional society? Was it seen perhaps as an unknown dimension with possible dangers for spiritual development? Were the new religious movements bent on affirming the traditional values connected to a monastic experience? Was Francis then one of many wishing a spiritual life and refusing the new society resulting from the widely adopted market economy? What was different in Francis that made of him the patron saint of Italy? Perhaps he did not really act differently from many others, except that at that particular historical moment, Gregory IX seriously needed the perfect saintly figure to brighten up the otherwise corroded Church's image. Can we say then that Francis was just one good willing hermit whose popularity was readily exploited by the Church? What would be a valid argument against this possibility?

There is no doubt that the Franciscan Order betrayed Francis' spirit. Already before his death the Order slowly took on a life of its own. Some historians justify the rejection of Francis'ideal by giving as a major factor the historical changes to which the Order had to adjust in its development. Supposedly, history changed and required the Order to be different from Francis' original intent. Here is an example:

> Organizations change; they have a history. Changes occurred among Francis and his brothers, among the sisters at San Damiano and within the associations of lay Franciscans. The changes developed their basic understandings, their practical decisions and their assessment of the result. The changes brought about a new set of circumstances, personal and institutional. That's life.[22]

There is a frightening sense of passivity and acceptance toward the historical happenings, as if an abstract force called "history" could command human ac-

---

20 Lester K. Little, "Evangelical Poverty, the New Money Economy and Violence" *Poverty in the Middle Ages*. Ed. David Flood. Franziskanische Forschungen 27 (Dietrich-Celde-Verlag, Werl/Westf., 1975): 11-26, here at 13.

21 Ibid., 15.

22 David Flood, *Work for Every One; Francis of Assisi and the Ethic of Service*. (Quezon City, Philippines: CCFMC for Asia/Oceania, Inter Franciscan Center, 1997), 127.

tions. We claim, then, that history changes, and so men and women change in accordance with it. Historians may find justifications and reasons condoning the most horrifying events in the name of historical necessity. The Franciscan Order became everything Francis would have refused: the basic idea so central to Francis' *forma vitae* practically disappeared. Who could give a thought to Francis' brilliant solution for social ills? Working with the *minores* without dealing with money or possessions, exchanging goods and services in perfect equality? It was only a dream.

Already during Francis' life many brothers resented his approach, so that Francis decided it was best for him to withdraw. Coming back from the Middle East in 1220, Francis was alarmed by the tension he found among the brothers. He resigned from his position as General Minister in favor of Pietro Cattani. Right after his death there were no obstacles to completely obliterating Francis' program by then considered according to a majority quite a crazy idea. The lack of recognition of the symbiotic effect of work and *paupertas* activated in a new kind of social relationship was one of the great misunderstandings of our history. Flood explains the circumstance of this misunderstanding:

> [...] those who took over the reins of the key Franciscan organization and those who have written about the change never recognized the centrality of work and did not because of the social determinisms in their own lives. Learned brothers who wrote and taught felt removed from toil, from the physical pains of daily labor.[23]

While Flood's comment is expressing precisely the situation, I believe there is more to it. Identifying Francis' idea of work simply with "the physical pains of daily labor" is misleading. Certainly labor had a bad reputation among all citizens in good standing. That it was seen as something diminishing to the dignity of social status is a well-known fact in European society still today, as we said before. However, Francis' emphasis is on the various activities, *ars*, already mastered by the brothers. Following the Gospel, Francis was encouraging the exercise of the brothers' natural talents and expertise, thus he did not expect the brothers to do exclusively manual work. The real reason why most brothers refused work as a central requirement is the fact clearly spelled out that they were not supposed to work for money or for any accumulation of material possessions. This was the critical point. It contradicted the social dynamic of their time.

Working without being paid with money when money was becoming the lifeblood of social life was unacceptable. At a time in which the money market was in full swing, taking hold of human heart and soul, Francis wanted the human heart to open wide to better realities, but the brothers were not up to the task. They opened their hearts to material power instead: they did not

---
23 Ibid., 129.

possess the quality of spirit Francis had hoped for. This is the reason why the Franciscan Order ended up being everything Francis would not have wanted. It was not because a necessary change was in order following the evolution of the market economy. It was not because no one in good social standing wanted to dedicate time to manual work. It was a refusal to acknowledge the intrinsic power and the real possibility of Francis' vision: the brothers loved the world and had no desire to change it. Instead they submitted passively and they were changed by it. The new wave of Franciscans transformed a lay community that enjoyed living in active peace sharing personal talent and alleviating each other's pains into a religious order dedicated to ascetic practices and to daily labor.

Why did Francis' emphasis on *ars* switch to labor? First, perhaps, because the brothers did not perceive the beauty of Francis' idea; thus, they actively tried to compensate for their lack of perception by choosing to give a different meaning to Francis' simple words. As a second step, they literally translated Francis' language into a more familiar one, more adaptable to their own reality. I do not believe it was done on purpose; it happened because of ignorance, in the same way it happens today, for example, among countries with different belief systems. Wars are the triumph of ignorance. And we are not talking of intellectual ignorance: it was, it is, ignorance of the heart. Once the word *ars* was translated into labor, it was easier to discard it, claiming the superiority of intellectual or of spiritual activities over "the physical pains of daily labor." The third and last step for the transformation of Francis' new world back into the older and more familiar environment involved the drastic separation between labor and *paupertas*: Francis' love, Lady *Paupertas*, changed into material poverty. It meant going back to the old monastic model of a religious community dependent on the Church's intervention, but this is precisely what the friars wanted: the simplicity and lightness of Francis' *forma vitae* were unbearable to the heavy materiality of their hearts. Francis' brotherhood changed its original structure because the brothers themselves wanted to transform it and actively created an environment more suitable to their brand of spirituality. The Franciscan community itself was busy making the Rule more flexible, glossing it according to convenience and twisting the meaning of Francis' concise language to serve a personal need for comfort. After Gregory IX, several popes were involved in the same operation, adapting and transforming the original intention into a cumbersome structure dedicated to the fulfillment of the Church's ministry. People make history by creating the situations they desire and by approving the social rules most favorable to their material needs. There is no higher force called "history" for determining people's actions. Human beings are in charge of this earth; they can make of it an earthly paradise, or they can drive it to catastrophe.

The transformation perceived during the last years of Francis' life increased its pace right after his death in 1226. Already before the canonization on July 16, 1228, Gregory IX had planned the construction of the basilica in Francis' honor thus indicating his intention in regard to the future of the Order. With *Mira circa nos,* three days after Francis' canonization, Gregory IX gave the real start to the papal program for the Franciscans. With inspired words and sincere hope Gregory defined his vision for what had to come:

> [...] behold, at the eleventh hour, he (the Lord) raised up his servant Francis, a man truly after his own heart. He was a beacon whom the rich viewed with contempt, but whom God had prepared for the appointed time, sending him into his vineyard to root out the thorns and brambles after having put the attacking Philistines to flight, to light up the path to our homeland, and to reconcile people to God by his zealous preaching.[24]

Afterward, *Quo elongati* was the turning point that in 1230 transformed the essence of Francis' *forma vitae.* Since with this bull the Pope himself denied validity to Francis' *Testament* and interpreted the Rule to fit the friars' mundane taste, the continuation of Franciscan history was quickly on a slippery slope, where even the most faithful friar accepted at least some of the changes made as a *fait accompli.* The Church was eager to satisfy the friars' desire for a clear interpretation of Francis' intention and did so by simplifying and lessening the friars' responsibilities, because by now Francis' simple directions sounded too harsh. Without work the idea of poverty as first intended was not a realistic possibility, unless the Church itself could intervene and it did. Besides declaring that the brothers "are not bound by the Rule to observe the counsels of the Gospel"[25] Gregory IX introduced new factors that made a difference in the friars' lifestyle and initiated a long chain of further transformations. First, the Pope made sure to let the brothers know that he was aware of their spiritual weakness. From his words it seems he completely condoned and justified it as a normal state, even for someone dedicated to a spiritual life: "[...] at times the Spirit discloses to your consciences what lies hidden to others. Still, because the darkness of human weakness beclouds the splendor of spiritual understanding, occasionally the anxiety of doubt presents itself and thus difficulties that are almost insurmountable begin to pile up."[26] The Pope's statement placed the friars, fallible human beings, at a distance from their spiritually superior founder: this theme will develop in time with great consequence. Next, the papal bull defined clearly how the friars could have the use of money and property while still respecting the vow of poverty. Already suggested with the

---

24 *Early Documents*, I, 566.

25 Ibid., 572.

26 *Francis of Assisi, Early Documents*, I, 570.

invention of the "spiritual friends" in the Later Rule chapter 4, this was indeed quite an accomplishment that only Gregory IX's legal mind could achieve. In fact without "work," unless under the Church's protection, there was no other possibility for the brothers to survive except by begging. Francis allowed the brothers to beg in case of necessity, not as an activity that could substitute for work; but once the idea of working disappeared, begging became a common activity and an important issue in the direction of the Order. Gregory IX, however, does not mention begging in *Quo elongati*. The main issue in the Pope's mind at this time was the growing requirement for clerical ministry. In his bull, Gregory IX reiterated what was already mentioned in the Later Rule, chapter 9. He stated: "[...] the Rule forbids any of the brothers to preach to the people unless he has been examined and approved by the general minister and received from him the office of preaching. [...]"[27] The Pope's declaration suggests there were difficulties in the brothers' preaching activity. In fact, although at the beginning the friars had to limit themselves to penitential preaching, they often ran into trouble with local clerics who did not accept the intrusion into their churches. But Gregory had a very clear idea of the charismatic appeal the brothers could have if appropriately trained. The Franciscan Order was an invaluable tool that needed to be nurtured. During the 1230s Gregory IX sent letters to church leaders stressing his vision for the friars, emphasizing the importance of their ministry. On August 28, 1231, the Pope drafted the bull *Nimis iniqua* addressed to prelates in England, France and Germany in defense of the friars who were often attacked by clerics. In this document the right of the friars to preach, once examined and approved by the General Minister, is implied. A few years later in 1237, in *Quoniam abundavit,* the Pope published a clear statement in which the Franciscan Order became "a task force to implement the pastoral provisions of the Fourth Lateran Council."[28] At this point it was clear that the penitential preaching which characterized the early brotherhood had taken on a more defined shape in favor of the pastoral needs of the Church. Ministry, then, took all the available space previously dedicated to work and to a life shared with the local *minores*. This was a major break with Francis' *forma vitae*, because it entailed a series of drastic changes in the friars' daily life. First of all, the friars destined to be preachers were required to undergo a rigorous intellectual training at the university level, thus, there was no time for a constructive relationship and work exchange with the local society. Work was relegated mostly to menial necessities confined within the convent's walls. The friars grew more and more alienated from their work activity, since it was clear to them that their pastoral duty and ministry was by far superior to

---

27 Ibid., 574.
28 Ibid., 575.

the work requested by Francis in the Early Rule. By now even the memory of it was conveniently disappearing.

We saw before that there was already a different focus between the Early and Later Rule: the Early Rule's limpid statement on work and refusal to be paid with money becomes more ambiguous in the Later Rule. We know that in the last period of his life, since he had come back from the Middle East, Francis had trouble trying to bring back some of the estranged brothers: it was only the beginning. We now focus our attention on the subject of work in the *Commentary on the Rule* by Hugh of Digne, completed about thirty years after Francis' death. He honestly wanted to give a contribution to a renewed understanding of Francis' *forma vitae*. Or so he says.

WORK ON THE RULE'S COMMENTARY BY HUGH OF DIGNE[29]

In 1255 Hugh of Digne wrote a commentary on the Rule of 1223. We have information about Hugh in Salimbene's *Chronicle*: "He was one of the great clerics of the world, an eminent preacher, beloved of the clergy and the people, excellent in controversy and competent in everything."[30] Besides Salimbene's high opinion of him, Hugh shows in his commentary on the Rule that he is sincerely interested in finding out about the origin of the Franciscan movement and is willing to face a stark reality confronting the confusion spread among the brothers. Is his sincerity a rhetorical tool meant to make his writing more interesting? For whom was he writing? In the prologue he begins: "That I should review the purpose of the Rule according to the teaching of the ancients [...] was imposed on me by obedience precisely to fill the lack for this and to prevent the calumnies of our detractors which spare no one."[31] Who ordered him? This is not clear although there are speculations about it. Flood explains: "Hugh sought to clarify the Franciscan soul in the early 1250s. His commentary belongs to the responsible effort to right the Franciscan movement in 1252. Hugh's reference to the obedience under which he wrote anchors his pages historically."[32] Mainly, Hugh felt compelled by his superiors, perhaps John of Parma, to help safeguard the troubled reputation of the Order, whose right to existence was doubted by many.

Reading his work does not result in a clarification of the Rule; on the contrary we have a sense of the confusion affecting the Franciscan community. In

---
29 The text used throughout this writing is *Commentary on the Rule of the Lesser Brothers by Hugh of Digne*. Introduction by David Flood. To be published by the Franciscan Institute.

30 *XIIIth Century Chronicles*, Translated from Latin by Placid Herman (Chicago: Franciscan Herald Press, 1961), 245.

31 *Commentary on the Rule of the Lesser Brothers by Hugh of Digne*, 21.

32 Hugh of Digne's *Rule Commentary*. Ed. David Flood (Grottaferrata: Spicilegium Bonaventurianum, 1979), 59.

any case it is appalling that after only about thirty years much could already be lost concerning the meaning of the Rule. Thirty years is a short time for having already forgotten most of Francis' expectations for his brotherhood. By reading Hugh's work we have also a precise sense of a drastic change in the brothers' attitudes, a different scenario from the proposed life-style described in the Early Rule. Hugh refers to it many times, showing a genuine desire to understand what Francis meant, but Francis' spirit is long gone, and the memory of him even after so little time has faded away.

Hugh's anger is palpable in the prologue. He complains that the Rule is misinterpreted or distorted by many, making it impossible to go back to the true "teaching of the ancients (*Propositum regulae iuxta sententiae antiquorum* [33])." This word "ancients" or elders is interesting: many of these so-called ancients must have been still alive and with a fresh remembrance of their memorable life with Francis. Where were they?

What was happening in Hugh's time that obliterated the correct reading of the Rule? Was it such a difficult reading? Or did the complication derive precisely from it being too simple? It seems obvious from what has come down to us that Francis wrote for all people, including uneducated ones; anyone could have easily understood its content precisely because it was brief, simple and to the point, even though we noted that the Later Rule ended up being more ambiguous than the Early Rule, at least concerning the manner of working. The real confusion began when learned Franciscans saw it as their duty to gloss and explain the Rule in their own way according to their more sophisticated understanding. We all know how much a well-educated person cherishes finding arguments for advancing subtle interpretations and provoking endless debates, all essential food for the brain. Learning has its dark side, as every human endeavor does. What happened within the brotherhood was exactly what Francis had anticipated when he wrote a warning in his *Testament* prohibiting any gloss to his Rule. Hugh is vaguely aware of Francis' warning. He writes: "The saint is believed to have sometimes forbidden these glosses, but not the necessary explanations about the truth."[34] Why would it have been "necessary" to explain the truth? It would seem that in the effort to mentally understand Francis' intention, people began reading into it more than what was really necessary. The point is that the simplicity of the Rule and its possible reverberating effect on the surrounding social environment was not appreciated or fully understood except by the first few brothers who shared experiences with Francis. There is a clear trend. With the flourishing of the Parisian university, the Church required an intellectual education for the friars destined to preaching and caring for laypeople. The need to exercise the mind activated also the

---
33 Ibid., 91.
34 *Commentary on the Rule of the Lesser Brothers*, 22.

drive for endless discussion and debates, which became a regular feature of university life. We can see this in the present university setting: in the best case we have much discussion and very little done; in the worst scenario, bad decisions are made with dire consequences for the health of the institution.

We are convinced that there was no reason for Francis to refuse learning; for example, he accepted it in the case of Anthony of Padua. The issue was not to despise education; rather, it was the excess, the misuse or abuse of it that was rightly to be avoided. May we assume a similar situation concerning Francis' refusal to use money? His pragmatism may have made him aware that money is a neutral force; it is neither good nor bad. However, at that historical moment in which coins and money were just starting to be used as normal exchange, there was danger for immoderate use at the service of greed and selfishness.[35] I can imagine that, in case of extreme emergency, Francis would have allowed the use of material power, of money, to help his brothers.

See how Hugh deals with the Rule concerning work and the compensation for it (Later Rule 4, 5, 6). In the first paragraph he states: "Note that a twofold manner of living is proposed in the Rule. The one through labor is proposed in this chapter, the other through alms in the following chapter. We can have recourse to spiritual friends, too, in case either come up short [...]" Was there a twofold manner of living expressed in the Rule? With his notation Hugh is showing that the essential part of the *forma vitae*, to work, had already undergone a deformation, because now it is considered of equal importance with begging. The refusal to consider work as a basic tool for living was already in process. To have recourse to alms was not an alternate equal choice for Francis; rather, it was an emergency measure for hard times when work was not sufficient for survival. Begging was the right of the poorest reaching for survival. Moreover, Hugh mentions only labor as a definition for work. We already pointed out that Francis' word, *ars*, imperfectly translated as *trade*, refers to many different kinds of occupations, all of which are useful to a sustainable community if accomplished with honesty, purity and good practical sense. In the last sentence Hugh claims the possibility to have recourse for help to a spiritual friend. The Later Rule in 1223, chapter 4, allowed counting on spiritual friends, benefactors, for most urgent needs such as clothing, food or shelter "according to places, seasons and cold climates." Gregory IX had softened the rule, devising legal solutions, but every solution created further ambiguity: benefactors often preferred to give money instead of other kinds of gifts. Gregory's answer was the introduction of a new element, an agent,

---

35 Coins is in Latin *denarius* and "was the primary means of exchange at the market [...]." Money or pecunia refers to "the wealth a person possessed, especially in his/her cattle or other goods. [...] it also means money in general [...] the whole system of money that was in circulation at the time." See Michael Cusato, "Poverty and Prosperity: Franciscans and the Use of Money" *Washington Theological Union* Symposium Papers (2009), 30.

nuntius, who could receive money for the friars, in case money was the easiest way. Of course it was. In order to hide the betrayal of the Franciscan spirit, a clever legal expedient made the *nuntius* an agent of the benefactor not of the friars. The spiritual friends were not so spiritual after all, considering that they were just an expedient for the material well-being of the brothers, a clever ruse allowing the Order to claim a life of evangelical poverty.

At the end of his reasoning Hugh reaches a conclusion that was also the official one recognized by the Order. Practically he states that the grace of working can come in different shapes, and with this assertion he puts corporal and spiritual work in the same basket observing, however, that: "... the spiritual work, as the better, excuses from corporal work." He has reached here a complete fusion with the general practice. In fact, his next citation is from St. Bernard: "As the saint says, *As much as the spirit surpasses the body, spiritual practices are more fruitful than corporal work.*"[36] With the introduction of St. Bernard we are back to a concept of the monastic lifestyle intruding into Franciscan practice; but the *forma vitae* was never meant to be confined within a convent's walls. Hugh's reliance on St. Bernard shows that the main purpose of the Franciscan community had ceased to exist: it was no more connected to the idea of a new community fully operating in the world. Instead, the Order was now oriented toward a more familiar structure identified with traditional monasticism that had given support in the past to an extraordinary flourishing of spirituality. Francis' concept, however, had a very different scope. He and his companions did not live in a fixed place; they worked in complete equality with the poorest and less fortunate members of their society. They lived "in the world," though in opposition to its current materialism. By citing St. Bernard of Clairvaux, builder of a monastic community, Hugh instead implies his favoritism for the monastic system in which a privileged group of people operated in an enclosed and controlled space under the Church's protective umbrella. For them body and spirit were two forces in tension, the spirit being superior to the other. For Francis, spirituality and corporality were united to form a unique model for a new humanity. Hugh is going back in time defining spirituality and corporality as two antagonistic energies in competition with each other. The old argument, whether Martha is better than Mary or vice versa, is in order. Hugh explains: "The trusted and prudent servant knows when to minister to the Lord sometimes in the role of Mary, at others that of Martha...."[37] This is a good thought; however, Mary and Martha are still opposed to each other. In fact, as the Masters have written, the brothers can use one or the other at

---

36 Ibid., 74.
37 Ibid.

different times to justify their lack of sincerity in their practice:[38] "Under the pretext of this passage, carnal brothers want to defend their laziness by saying that the spirit of prayer is extinguished whenever superiors impose some work upon them...."[39] Hugh rightly argues that, though Martha and Mary correspond to different gifts, they should be kept in a good balance and used at the proper time, because nothing can be done without both acting in harmonious cooperation. The main problem in Hugh's argument is identifying the spiritual activity with prayer and the corporal one with work. This is a complete reversal of Francis' principles. Work and prayer, body and soul, were completely coinciding: in his *forma vitae* Francis overcame the dualistic approach typical of social values. Work was also a spiritual activity as was prayer: work was prayer, a celebration of human potential and spiritual life. No one understood better than Francis; many of his brothers, Hugh and his contemporaries could not.

The split between work and preaching or doing spiritual things is clear in Hugh's commentary because the preoccupation is more focused now on the problem of poverty. To maintain the vow of poverty became a real problem once work was not the central point in the friars' lives any more. Thus all the issues related to poverty became paramount in the friars' search for truth. One of the most discussed issues was then the problem of ownership as it is strictly connected to evangelical poverty. How was it possible to be poor and still have ownership of material things? There is obvious incongruence between the two concepts, and the possibility of fitting one into the other required intellectual prowess. When Hugh ventures to describe the different kind of ownership a brother can afford, his reasoning is increasingly convoluted. He cites extensively from the Four Masters' commentary, which is by now the standard measure for the friars' theoretical activity, but he does not seem to be able to make good sense out of it. He barely reports what others say or believe, testifying to a wide divergence of opinion among his brothers. The following quotations exemplify his doubts on how to deal with the subject of ownership related to possession of material necessary for work. He points out that different types of material require different approaches: "[…] some materials have no price and […] the whole value comes to it from the art, such in mats and baskets which are made from rushes […] and is to be classed as to no one's good. But materials that can be priced, such as hides, leather and cloth […] they (the brothers) may not receive because their possession carries ownership with it."[40] He quotes the explanation from the Masters but does not seem convinced

---

38 Between 1241-1242, four Franciscan scholars wrote the *Expositio Quatuor Magistrorum* (Edited by L. Oliger. Rome: Edizioni di Storia e Letterartura, 1950), a commentary on the Rule. The Four Masters were Alexander of Hale, John of La Rochelle and probably Eudes Rigaud and Robert of La Basse. Their commentary became the most used reference for all other Franciscan scholars.

39 *Commentary on the Rule of the Lesser Brothers*, 74.

40 Ibid., 76.

because in the next paragraph he asks questions about possible arrangement in order to avoid ownership: "If they can work with worthless materials, how will such handicrafts (be valued), since they (the brothers) cannot sell the finished product either personally or through others? [...] a thing considered no good to anyone by whose authority will it be sold?" He clarifies his question by stating what was usually done, that is to sell it "under the authority of the lord of the place" or "when no one seems to be the owner, under the authority of the Apostolic See which has assumed the ownerships of the things the Order uses."[41] Hugh's indecision establishing a clear praxis for the friars' commercial operations indicates the actual disorientation dominating the religious communities. Transactions involving money through spiritual friends must have been already a common occurrence, but were often seen with suspicion. Hugh also states at the end that there used to be another way to exchange goods and this one was the one favored by the "ancients." He explains that the brothers could "exchange such things for others necessary for their lives, whose acquisition from their labor is granted through the Rule. [...] And this custom the ancients held in highest esteem." This is finally an acknowledgement of a real statement in the Early Rule: the brothers were exchanging their work for what they needed in their lives. They did not use money as payment. Right after, in the final paragraph of chapter 5, what he had just said is lost in translation: in fact Hugh repeats what he thought Francis would have wished: "[...] to have recourse not to dispute but to alms [...] if ever the wage for their labor was not forthcoming."[42] The original Latin reads: "[...] *non ad litem sed ad eleemosynam ut tactum est recurrere voluit, si quando laboris pretium non daretur.*"[43] In the original Latin *pretium* has a wider meaning than *wage*. It may mean price, value or reward while the modern English *wage* refers mostly to money given for labor or services. The assumption of the translation into English is that the brothers' recompense for their labor is a payment in money while in fact the Latin is more flexible. Recall that the Latin *labor* includes a possible variety of jobs, while the English *labor* refers more strictly to manual work. It would seem that the turmoil generated by the erroneous interpretation of the Rule in Hugh's time is compounded by the lack of clarity of the modern translation. In any case the problems detected in the use of language testify to a change of position vis-à-vis the Rule, already starting during Francis' lifetime, and increasing rapidly after his death.

It is clear that the Franciscan environment had already been manipulated in order to adapt to social convenience. It was enough to cause plenty of incomprehension and doubt among the brothers. Hugh, though seemingly pro-

---

41   Ibid., 76.
42   Ibid., 77.
43   Flood, 144.

foundly keen to the honest discovery of truth, is also distant from the Rule's original approach. We face an impossible situation because we discover that Francis had lived truly in a different existential dimension. He planted the seeds of a spiritual comprehension that was far from blooming at his time just as in ours. It is pointless to follow Hugh in his search for lost meanings. In any case it is surprising that only thirty years after Francis' demise, his truth and the chance to succeed in creating a humane society could be completely forgotten by the very people participating in it. Or perhaps was it waiting to be proposed again at a later time? Is it still waiting for men and women capable of speaking and acting with simplicity and transparency as Francis did?

The change of mentality among the brothers was certainly not a natural biological evolution of the human species, though sometimes it looks so in the writing of modern historians, the ones eager to justify the Order for its lack of faith in Francis' *forma vitae*. It is true that the 1230 papal bull published by Gregory IX, *Quo elongati*, authorized a first drastic and determinant change, but this was not just the Pope's decision. Most brothers were in agreement with the Pope judging the Rule by far too hard for them. Gregory IX was interpreting the wish clearly manifested by the brothers and, in the interest of the Church, thought it best to satisfy their request. It was already evident during the last years of Francis' life that several brothers - the clerics - were refusing to follow the path indicated in the *forma vitae*. In this regard Hugh shows his own incertitude: he is not able to decide the best way to deal with the friars' economy, torn between the recompense they deserve for their work and the cumbersome system created by the Church for keeping alive the idea of *paupertas* required by the Rule.

After Hugh's chapter 5 dedicated to *The Manner of Working*, chapter 6 deals with money and possession, which directly relates to *paupertas*. It is the longest chapter, 24 pages, to testify that the content was of primary interest for the friars, constantly preoccupied now by the question of poverty to which the Order was theoretically dedicated. "Let the brothers not make anything their own" was Francis' message. To avoid ownership sounded at first such a simple concept in Francis' words, but it turned out to be a most complex state of affairs, practically unachievable by the brothers in the thirteenth century or ever after. Again, we need to keep in mind that at this point in the Order's history the connection between work and *paupertas* as advocated by Francis in the Early Rule had already lost its primary role in the brothers' daily lives. In following the brotherhood's evolution toward an increasing distance from Francis' *forma vitae*, the vow for evangelical poverty became highly problematic and the subject of sophisticated academic arguments.

Hugh proceeds in order, trying to answer the main questions. "What making their own means" he asks. And secondly he formulates what seems to be a rhetorical question: "whether those contracts that involve ownership are allowed [...], such as buying, selling, lending, contracting, renting, exchanging, pledging, mortgaging, and donating."[44] It seems strange that he could ask such a question, because the answer can only be a resounding "no, they cannot." But he must have his reason; mainly, while he is committed to finding the truth, he also delights in sophisticated reasoning as some Franciscans of his age did. Francis' simple statements were not in tune with the new mentality. The third of Hugh's doubts was "whether while the ownership of things is excluded, their use be freely permitted." But the most important, the basic question is the fourth one: "what is that poverty to which the brothers are bound?" Hugh abundantly uses the Four Masters to answer his questions. The discourse is ever more subtle in order to justify the fact that the friars, protected and nourished by the Holy See, were perhaps never really poor. It is most interesting to know how Hugh answers the two main questions. The first has to do with ownership: "making their own." He writes, following the Masters:

> Ownership is the right of mastery... Anyone who has such rights over his goods, even if he possesses nothing corporeal is not poor, because from these incorporeal rights he is able to attain to the ownership of corporal goods whether mobile or immobile. And for that reason to have these is incompatible with a vow to have nothing.[45]

However, the remedy to the conflict between poverty and ownership is quickly found: "...They can act through any faithful person who is instructed beforehand... such a one does this for the sake of the brothers, he does not do by their authority since he knows that they are bound by no obligation either to him or to others; they would thus be bound if he were to do it on their authority."[46] The problem is cleared in regard to ownership while all other obstacles to possession are also resolved with some more subtleties. Answering the question "what is the poverty to which the brothers are bound" requires a long discourse for which Hugh borrows heavily from the Masters. He defines different degrees of poverty: one is a "certain less perfect poverty" which has nothing superfluous but retains what is necessary, the other one is a "more perfect poverty" which has nothing at all, superfluous or necessary, relying completely on divine providence. This last one is the poverty of the *Fratres Minores*; Hugh calls it "extreme poverty." The immediate consequence of the extreme poverty, however, is begging. He says: "For begging is the sign of true poverty."[47] Hugh follows closely the Early Rule for his discussion on begging. He says: "For begging when the necessity of poverty urges is licet; when ne-

---
44 Ibid., 79.
45 Ibid., 80.
46 Ibid., 82.
47 Ibid., 94.

cessity is lacking, it is illicit."[48] It follows an explanation of why brothers must not feel ashamed to beg. But noticing the effort Hugh makes trying to clarify and justify the act of begging, we realize that begging had taken the central place, claiming an absolute importance over any other work activity. Certainly this was not present in Francis' Rule. The intention in the Rule specifies that in case work was not sufficient for sustenance, the brothers could go for alms. It was not an imperative, but an occasional need dictated by unfortunate circumstances. The extreme poverty claimed by Hugh and his Masters had the unavoidable company of begging; thus, it forced the brothers into an impossible gimmick, alienating them from their social environment. Soon both the population and the clergy began despising the mendicants' intrusion into the city ecclesial life. No wonder friars like Hugh were asked by their superiors to write in order to dispel the Order's bad reputation and the "calumnies of detractors which spare no one."[49]

It is necessary to show to which extent the work issue was not really an issue anymore. It had disappeared from the friars' concern, replaced by the duty of ministry and by begging. It does not have any space in their discussions. No one needed to be involved in a real practical occupation. The only kind of work suitable to the friars was the ministry, and for whoever wanted to practice the fullness of evangelical poverty there was begging. Hugh goes on writing for several pages. It may be recognizable to the reader that he is mentioning a situation within the Order. For example, continuing his discourse on poverty he admonishes: "[…] how will we be poor unless we patiently put up with need for the Lord's sake? The truly poor man not only bears need with a calm spirit when it occurs, but accepts its even constant practice by living always frugally and temperately."[50] The idea of "putting up with need" was not the same as the simplicity of spirit accompanying an active and joyous day of work; rather, it was a passive expectation of the constant practice of an ascetical, material poverty that tortures body and spirit.

We found Hugh of Digne's commentary on the Rule fraught with indecision and incomprehension. His attempt to clarify the Rule achieves the opposite result. The issues of work and *paupertas* proposed by Hugh are incompatible with the freshness of Francis' *forma vitae*. His effort eloquently expresses the profound disarray suffered by the Order; however, we notice also that Hugh is at ease with his time. In his writing, we do not find any polemic or element contrary to the Church's decisions. But while he is useful for our understanding of Franciscan history, he is no help for knowing more about Francis and his companions, even though he is living at quite a short time distance from

---

48 Ibid.
49 This is what Hugh affirms in the prologue to his commentary on the Rule, 21.
50 Ibid.

Francis's death when several of his closest brothers were still alive. We could deduce that, given the new mentality and cultural atmosphere, the Franciscan brothers were not interested anymore in Francis as a person. He was already only a myth.

We leave now Hugh of Digne in the good company of the Four Masters, and we begin our inquiry on work and the Rule's commentary by brother Peter of John Olivi, reputed to be the most learned friar of his time. Was he closer than Hugh of Digne to Francis' truth and to his companions? Was his powerful intelligence capable of penetrating the by now esoteric quality of Francis' Rule? As for Hugh of Digne, our intention is to find out Olivi's approach to the issue of work and its relation with Franciscan *paupertas*.

WORK AND *USUS PAUPER*: PETER OF JOHN OLIVI

Work did not constitute a problem anymore, simply because in the evolution of the order it had lost its place. In Olivi's time (1248-1298) the main Franciscan issue was certainly the interpretation of poverty that, for the friars who followed the original *forma vitae,* coincided with the concept of *minoritas,* while for a majority of Franciscans it was increasingly narrowed down to material poverty with a legal interpretation of ownership officially approved by papal authority. Poverty, in any case, was part of the Franciscan vowed life, and as such it constituted a particularly sensitive issue for all Franciscans. Bonaventure also made an important intervention in 1269 with his *Apologia pauperum,* followed by John Pecham's *Apologia pauperis contra insipientem* and Thomas Aquina's *De perfectione vitae spiritualis*. By now *paupertas* was the Franciscan issue par excellence. The work issue had already been apparently resolved as we already explained; however, it was revisited by the Spirituals who expected the brothers to go back to the original intent. We could note at this point that, as we understand "Francis' original intent," it was probably somewhat blurred in the brothers' memory on both sides: the Community (followers of papal authority) and the Spirituals faithful to Francis.[51] In any case, even though the commitment to work did not constitute a problem anymore within the Order, the Rule's requirement for poverty kept haunting the brothers' consciences. Characteristically, the debate became abstract and theological, focusing now more on intention than on a practical way of life.

As work lost its original central place in Franciscan life, *paupertas* became ever more indefensible. It became the main issue in the organization of the Order, while everything related to work was put to rest and apparently resolved. Olivi was probably the only one to find an acceptable, rational way to explain how poverty could function in everyday practice. He wrote extensive-

---

51 Let us be aware that the terms Community and Spirituals are anachronistic in Hugh's time. They were not used until around 1310.

ly on the subject, provoking an intense debate in the *usus pauper* controversy. While protest was intensifying in Italy, in France Peter of John Olivi was stirring interest among friars with his interpretation of *usus pauper*, literally poor or restricted use. Olivi theoretically exposed the contested issue apparently with a clear understanding of Francis' spiritual conviction. Even though he did not mean to support the protests of the Spirituals, nevertheless he was later to be adopted by them as a leader in the *usus pauper* controversy. He was attacked and censured by the Order during the generalate of Jerome of Ascoli (1274-79) and later on, even after his death. In the intellectual environment of his time his work on *usus pauper* has been most important for determining the structure within which the Franciscan Order developed. In particular the relationship among the Church, the leadership of the Order and the movement of the Spirituals is strictly connected with Olivi's interpretation of *usus pauper*. It is essential then to understand the development of the debate on poverty formulated by Olivi. There is great interest in Olivi among modern scholars today; his versatility has caused various and often intriguing interpretations, because it is possible to find different angles to consider in Olivi's theoretical discussion. Before examining his *Commentary of the Rule of the Lesser Brothers*, in which we find a specific discussion of the work issue, we will seek help for a clarification of Olivi's concept of *usus pauper* from scholars who studied his work in depth.

David Burr has analyzed Olivi's view with an objective eye, illustrating in detail his interpretation of the *Questions on Evangelical Perfection* (early 1279) and *The Treatise on usus pauper*, completed between late 1279 and 1283. Olivi was very active between the 1270s and the 1280s, with most of his work dated during that period while he was also teaching. In fact, in his writing, the format related to the lectures given to his students is evident. Olivi's preoccupation with the subject of poverty testifies to the continuing struggle within the Franciscan Order over the restricted use of material resources. In his interpretation Burr notices that Olivi, in the course of the *Questions*, "considers practically every imaginable argument for the superiority of wealth and provides some sort of response from the Christian perspective."[52] Olivi considered poverty to be the central issue for the Franciscan Order, not an idealistic concept that could be separated from daily life: the commitment to *usus pauper* was supposed to be a Franciscan vow just like obedience and chastity. For Olivi poverty is absolutely central, so much so that a slight distancing from its practice would mean a victory for the forces of evil. This was the crucial point of Olivi's interpretation.

---

52 David Burr, *The Persecution of Peter Olivi* (Philadelphia: The American Philosophical Society, 1976), 12.

Once more it is important to point out the growing complexity of the argumentation necessary to deal with the Franciscan vow of poverty once work had lost its space in the friars' activity. The disappearance of work created an unrecognized unbalance that could not be cured by theoretical arguments. Olivi, however, provided the most sophisticated intellectual construction of his time, something that still today can be considered a marvel of perfect reasoning. For a while it filled the void left by the disappearance of work.

In the fifth of the *Questions on Evangelical Perfection,* Olivi "asks whether is better to perform an act with or without a vow and decides for the former."[53] After his clear statement for the positive value of the vow, Olivi takes into consideration some strong views which oppose his affirmation, namely that a vow places an individual in danger of sin if the vow is broken, that a vow denies the possibility of acting voluntarily, that forbidding what was previously permissible would increase the sinful desire for it and finally, that Christ never mentioned the necessity of a vow. Olivi answers all the points giving to each of them a positive value. In the first case the merit consists in the value of what is renounced and certainly freedom has the highest value. Burr explains: "the merit of a vow in Olivi's eyes depends upon the fact that freedom is simultaneously given and retained in it."[54] An individual renounces his freedom by vowing, but also is still capable of free choice in the future in a multiplicity of voluntary acts. The fact that *usus pauper* is included in the vow means that each person has the freedom to decide what is the proper action in each particular circumstance, adapted to the singularity of each person. Sylvain Piron clarifies this concept by explaining that the vow requires the voluntary and continued renunciation of the will, in which case will and freedom coincide; will is the principal element directing a person who then becomes completely free, as far as s/he is in complete control of the will, and thus s/he has "free will."[55] These are beautiful words and the concept seems to have solved all human quandaries about the rigorous quality of the vow: its rigor is sublimated by freedom of choice. But, as Piron rightly comments, this requires also a personal commitment because the vow must be understood as the highest form of self-mastery. As such it does not seem to be an exercise afforded by a great majority of people. It appears to be a greater responsibility than simply being

---

53 Ibid., 12.

54 Ibid.

55 Sylvain Piron, « Perfection évangélique et moralité civile : Pierre de Jean Olivi et l'étique économique franciscaine» *Ideologia del credito fra tre e quattrocento : dall'Astesano ad Angelo da Chivasso.* Eds. Barbara Molina and Giulia Scarcia, 103-43. Collana del centro studi sui Lombardi e sul credito nel Medioevo, 3 (Asti: 2001), 107 : "Le voeu de lui-même, possède une valeur propre, indexée sur celle de la volonté libre dont il constitue l'abdication volontaire et continuée. En identifiant volonté et liberté, l'anthropologie olivienne transforme la notion, traditionnelle dans l'école franciscaine, du primat de la volonté, pour en faire la structure réflexive d'un pouvoir sur soi par lequel la personne humaine peut se constituer en entité pleinement consistante, et libre dans la mesure où elle se possède elle-même. »

told what precisely one is supposed to do, without leaving the choice to every single person. Certainly there is the danger of breaking the vow without even knowing, but this may happen only if the person is not spiritually trained to recognize a real necessity versus what instead would constitute an overstep into laxity. With the vow, then, individual responsibility and freedom of choice are emphasized without denying natural necessity. But who really wants freedom when it is accompanied by harsh responsibility tied to a vow that, if broken, might mean eternal damnation?

Olivi's statement about the necessity of including *usus pauper* in the vow stressed the importance of individual responsibility. As a consequence, in perfect harmony with the Franciscan spirit, there was also an emphasis on refusing to obey orders clearly contrary to conscience: "There was little place in such a world for Olivi's notion that the friar had the responsibility to disobey superiors if they demanded violation of the rule."[56] This, of course, was not pleasing to clerical authorities. Other issues concerning Olivi's apocalyptic vision attracted so many followers that the Church felt obliged to inquire about his activity. The struggle focuses on Provence where Olivi's influence, even after his death in 1298, gained ground among friars and also among the laity, despite the confiscation of his writings and the punishment of those who refused to hand them over, or perhaps precisely because of it, since persecution encouraged a contrary reaction. His doctrine of *usus pauper* is understood as essential to the Franciscan vow; for Olivi the vow of poverty was the cornerstone upon which Franciscan spiritual life was built, in accordance with the mystery of Christ's Incarnation.[57] On the other hand, John of Murrovalle, the new minister general appointed by Boniface VIII, called *usus pauper* "an alien and wrongheaded teaching." In 1317 John XXII, in his battle against the Spirituals, included also Olivi, whose tomb in Narbonne was desecrated; in 1319 his Apocalypse commentary was censured by a papal commission and also by a Franciscan general chapter.

Modern commentators on Olivi are often creative in their approach. David Flood sees Olivi from a different angle with respect to Burr's objective eye. In his article on Peter of John Olivi he is concerned about Olivi's social agenda. Concerning the *Questions on Evangelical Perfection* number eight, Flood affirms that Olivi is interpreting *usus pauper* as the possibility of a social reformation and is encouraging his brothers to follow the Rule, which corresponds precisely to living life by the Gospel. Flood states for example: "[…] Whereas Parisian masters taught doctrine, Brother Peter proposed action. He was a Franciscan and not a theologian.[…] QPE VIII (*Questions on Evangelical*

---

56 David Burr, *Olivi and Franciscan poverty*. (Philadelphia: University of Pennsylvania, 1989), 194.

57 Piron, ibid., 108-109 : « Si la perfection évangélique consiste bien à vivre au plus près de l'Incarnation, la pauvreté en est la pierre angulaire. »

Perfection number eight) lies at the heart of Olivi's lectures. It turns his idea of Franciscan life into a practical program."[58] This perspective was not emphasized in Burr's commentary. On the contrary, Burr states: "Olivi was not only a Franciscan, but an intellectual as well. By the late 1270s he was a lector with a growing reputation in scholarly circles."[59] It would seem that Flood is consistently interested in social awareness. This is certainly a worthwhile direction, but in Olivi's case it is not possible to disagree with Burr: Olivi is an intellectual and a great one, a theologian, a philosopher, and also, as we will see next, an expert in economics. He is indeed a figure larger than life.

In fact, with a fantastic jump Giacomo Todeschini perceives Olivi as an economist. As he writes in the preface to his book: "The entire discourse sounded paradoxical. The idea that professionals of poverty had analyzed the market and the formation of prices seemed to be a quite extravagant fantasy since it was not customary for either Catholics or Marxists to mix the sacred with the profane."[60] According to Todeschini, Olivi was one of the first Franciscans to deal with economics, the market and exchange, and he is particularly important for his strict adherence to the Franciscan spirit while being knowledgeable of the mercantile reality of his homeland, Provence. Southern France was a particularly active region where, in a mix of different cultures characterized also by the deep-rooted presence of Jewish communities, commercial ventures flourished. Olivi taught in Narbonne and later at the Franciscan school in Montpellier, a city with an intense commercial life. According to Todeschini, Olivi first manifested an inclination toward understanding basic principles of economy when in the 1270s he was writing the *Questions on Evangelical Perfection,* mostly the eighth, ninth and tenth questions: he was confronted by the subject of the relative value of movable and immovable goods. After about ten years, while in Montpellier, he was faced with problems connected with the local mercantile economy, and around 1294 in Narbonne he wrote a treatise on commerce and usury, a minor work that has not attracted much attention among scholars.[61] The concern for economics, however, was already visible in the *Questions*. Todeschini affirms that, in the ninth question, discussing poverty as a primary Christian value, Olivi: "[...] defined voluntary poverty as a technique for using things based on the knowledge of their specific

---

58 David Flood, "The Theology of Peter John Olivi" *The History of Franciscan Theology.* Ed. Kenan Obsborne (St. Bonaventure, New York: The Franciscan Institute, 2007); 127-184, here at 159.

59 Burr, *The Persecution of Peter Olivi* , 24.

60 Giacomo Todeschini, *Franciscan Wealth. from Voluntary Poverty to Market Society*, Trans. Donatella Melucci (St. Bonaventure, New York: The Franciscan Institute, 2009), 7.

61 Pierre de Jean Olivi, ed. S. Piron, "Marchands et confesseurs: le traité des contracts d'Olivi dans son context." *L'argent au Moyen Age* (Paris: Sorbonne, 1998), 289-308.

usefulness."[62] The effort consists in being able to understand and separate what is a basic necessity from the superfluous.

If Olivi's interest in economy is historically contextualized, it becomes evident that the material condition of his time and place were certainly consonant to such reflection. After all, the new mercantile or commercial profit economy was blooming in southern France creating a dynamic, but also confusing environment, particularly for the friars who were committed to Franciscan poverty: as the context shifts, so too does the content of spirituality. It made sense for Olivi to find a place for *paupertas* in a system that was based entirely on material profit. Again Todeschini rightly argues: "[...] Olivi discussed poverty and wealth because he was a Franciscan from Languedoc [...] learned in theology and law, and an erudite expert of mercantile realities like those in southern France [...]"[63]

A main obstacle haunting the Franciscan community confronted Olivi: the separation between the use of money and its possession. If money is not considered as valuable and desirable in itself, but only as a price for providing something useful, "it does transform itself into an entity that passes among people without definitively belonging to any of them."[64] Olivi considered perverse and sinful the desire to take possession of coins as of something precious in itself: in the Early Middle Ages, however, coins did have an intrinsic value in themselves, because they were made of precious material and the tendency to accumulate them was quite natural. For Olivi, though, coins must have a purely symbolic function; they are an arbitrary sign reflecting the value of a needed object. This impersonality of money, its exclusive functionality destined to provide only for the necessities of human life, constituted the basis for his speculation on *usus pauper*. The poverty of the friars is proposed by Olivi as a measure of evaluation for identifying the real value of need and necessity. The study and in-depth analysis of the Rule that made Franciscan poverty almost feasible in the mercantile economy brought Olivi to participate with Pope Nicholas III in the promulgation of a bull related to it, *Exiit qui seminat* of 1279. Certainly, the actual practice required purity of intention and of action, and probably it did not happen often that Franciscan communities could live up to the rigorous demand of *paupertas*, as interpreted by Olivi's *usus pauper*.

But there is a piece obviously still missing in the analysis of Franciscan poverty, a piece that was not taken into consideration, not even by the careful study done by Peter of John Olivi. We saw that in Hugh's commentary the concept of work as intended in Francis' *forma vitae* had disappeared; no one seemed to be interested in the important place Francis had given to work

---

62 Todeschini, ibid., 95.
63 Ibid., 94.
64 Ibid., 100.

in the community. The concern was directed toward the issue of poverty and begging. In Olivi's case his elaborate theory of *usus pauper* is completely disconnected from the idea of work. We have to examine his *Commentary on the Rule* in order to establish his approach to the Franciscan work issue.

In his prologue to the Rule's commentary Olivi explicitly states: "... to give a brief and easy guide to it for the more simple, we want to investigate briefly the literal content and development of the said Rule and its correct, pure and simple meaning in a spirit of true and singular simplicity."[65] The first thing to notice is Olivi's style, very well organized in the evident effort to make his explanation simple. He does not succeed, because what he ends up doing is dissecting words and meanings in subtle details and distinguishing parts of discourse in need of further clarification: in fact a very complex procedure. But our interest is in his comment on chapter 4 on "evangelical poverty." It jumps to the reader's attention that he identifies right away, without the slightest hesitation, work with "labor or work with their hands."[66] Afterward, a long citation from the Four Masters helps him to explain that every type of exchange can be used as money (*pecunia*). After first noting that money is "necessary" he writes: "Secondly, in the fifth chapter he (Francis) introduces something to take its place in getting what is necessary, namely, labor or work of their hands." He also admits that there is another way to get food and that is "by begging for alms as mendicants."[67] The rest of his comments on the subject of work and compensation are on nothing else but "money." He goes on dealing with the necessities for the sick brothers and very briefly refers to the "spiritual friend." The straightforward logic with which he assumes the necessity to have those friends is surprising: "He (Francis) saw well that for necessities money sometimes could and should be obtained without us having any ownership or handling of it. [...] But the declaration of Pope Gregory and Pope Nicholas treat adequately how without this it could be done lawfully through friends."[68] He is very confident as he is relying faithfully on the papal bulls and on the Four Masters, in sum, the authorities officially recognized by the Order. A more elaborate discourse on work is found on Chapter 5. His ideas on work and ownership do not differ greatly from what Hugh writes on his commentary. What is evident, though, is Olivi's theoretical mastery of the subject, the ability and sophistication with which he explains clearly all the various points of each question without losing for a moment the rigor of his argument. At about thirty years distance from Hugh, we found the same issues solidified

---

65 *Commentary on the Rule of the Lesser Brothers by Peter of John Olivi.* Ed. David Flood. To be published by the Franciscan Institute, 18.
66 Ibid., 50.
67 Ibid., 51.
68 Ibid., 53.

and taken for granted. By now Olivi and his contemporary Franciscans have an intense preoccupation with manual work. They alternate between the possibility of avoiding it altogether and the chance of being able to find a place for it in their daily activity, according to what the papacy has established with the many bulls expressly dedicated to them. The crucial point is that work is not anymore a mean of subsistence but just an occupation that helps the friars to overcome idleness, "the enemy of the soul." Here is a colorful comparison that demonstrates Olivi's eloquence: "For just as a hidden and silent evaporation and emission from burning coals, imperceptibly and quite suddenly takes away its fiery strength and reduces it completely to barren and useless ashes; so idleness imperceptibly and quite suddenly, extinguishes fervor of spirit and all the strength of the virtues."[69] He has an extraordinary literary talent and a great argumentative style, but we do not see that he truly understands Francis and the original *forma vitae* better than others. He missed the whole point of the necessity of work emphasized in the Early Rule.[70] He explains as it follows:

> [...] where it brings with it an evident and notable harm, then it is enjoined on him against his soul and Rule. [...] this is one of those cases, which one may see that one is not able to observe the Rule spiritually, and especially if the work is superfluous, not really necessary nor pious, not closely linked to spiritual things. No sane reason could say for what it would be lawful for the brothers to be distracted or to distract them from the spirit or fervor of devotion [...] [71]

As a consequence, it would be better for the brothers to avoid work that can be dangerous to their soul and dedicate themselves completely to "spiritual things." As in Hugh, here Francis is long gone. In fact, when he argues, as Hugh does, whether the words "may work" are to be understood as a precept, Olivi answers that yes, from Francis' intention and from what he wrote in his *Testament*, it would appear that indeed work is a precept. But immediately afterward, Olivi completely disregards what he had just affirmed to be Francis' intent, and with a sudden change of direction turns instead to the Pope's decision in the bull *Exiit qui seminat*. Olivi cites a long passage from the bull in order to substantiate the fact that the Pope has more weight in the decision making than Francis' original vision. For Olivi, as for all Franciscans, it was officially accepted that "[...] those engaged in study or in the divine services should be restricted, to manual labor, since the example of Christ and of many saints shows that spiritual work takes precedence, as much as matters concern-

---

69   Ibid., 56.
70   An interesting and important detail is that Olivi is using exclusively the Later Rule while Hugh referred more often to the Early Rule.
71   Ibid., 58.

ing the soul take precedence over bodily concerns."[72] Francis' *forma vitae* was forgotten, and now we have Olivi's powerful intellect defending and encouraging the Pope's interpretation.

It is clear that both the Franciscans and the Church supported a total makeover of Francis, an artificial construction that satisfied the Franciscans with a life of comfort and security under the Church's protection. It satisfied the Church as well, because, in a moment of great struggle for the endless competition with the Empire, it gave new luster to its political power helped by the success of a well-organized Franciscan Order.

In his argumentation Olivi refers extensively to Augustine's *De opera monachorum*; in so doing he is perfectly in tune with the official trend that would want to model the Franciscan Order on a more traditional religious structure. Concerning the issue of work, in fact, he most often quotes Augustine in order to explain his own approach. Having in mind his simple reader in need of a detailed explanation, his rhetoric unfolds, opening a variety of points that he considers carefully one by one. Having quoted from *Exiit qui seminat* demonstrating his agreement with papal decisions, he opens a discussion against "some spiteful people." He does not specify who these people are, but we know there were several.[73] Using also Augustine, they argue against Olivi bringing up three points: first, that one who has no means of support has an obligation (precept) to do manual work; second, that prayer, study or preaching do not justify a lack of manual work; third, that it is better for them to work with their hands than not to work. A fourth point argues that "it is imprudent and presumptuous, or at least imperfect, to expose oneself to the dangers of begging."[74] Olivi's counter argument against Gerard de Abbeville and his friends takes several pages; he gives his adversaries four choices, and then he goes on explaining each of them with different points. To answer the first one he develops a "sevenfold clear argument against them." The expression "it is clear that" keeps repeating throughout his counterargument, in which he affirms common assumptions in his society that do not at all reflect Francis' intention. For example: "... it will be more useful to pray and meditate on divine things and study and read and preach than to be occupied with manual work..." and "... the above works are by their nature higher and better than bodily work...." Later he argues that sometimes there is a reason for enforcing the precept for doing manual work, and this time he quotes from "the words of the Apostle" who "laid this down only for those who, because of their restlessness, idleness, greed and spiritual weakness, were not able to hold back in any other good way from the evils...."

---

72 Ibid., 60. Please note that this translation has not been completely edited and there may be some imprecision in the use of language.

73 In the note n.124, 60, we read that these people were probably from the circle of Gerard de Abbeville.

74 Ibid., 62.

Again this idea belongs to the typical mindset governing the organization of monastic orders. Another example is particularly striking and certainly at the opposite end of the Franciscan spirit: he mentions that when Augustine says that Paul wanted the servants of God to work, Paul was in fact referring only to a particular group of people, and later Augustine declares "that Paul commands this for *those who do not have the power which he had.*" Moreover, Olivi argues: "According to the text of Augustine, the Apostle in 1 Corinthians 9:4-6 says that he and Barnabas had the power not to work because they had the power to eat and to be accompanied by a woman" And he goes on further explaining: "… we say, firstly, that Paul had the power not to work, not only because as a prelate he had the right to demand necessary provisions, but also because as a preacher he had the power to eat and to have a travelling companion."[75] With these statements Olivi approves and reinforces the Order's hierarchic structure; this does not fit at all with Francis' expectation for his new community in which there is complete equality of status and action among the brothers. For precision, Olivi adds that what he has just said about "power" would not be the only reason for not working; there are many others, and his argument keeps expanding, embracing every possible counterargument. Augustine, the Apostle and the Pope are on his side. Responding to whoever says that prayer, study and preaching do not excuse from working, he clarifies that Augustine never intended to affirm that those activities never excuse one from working, but that only in some cases and also not all persons in equal manner. He writes:

> [...] What argument is to say that if we are not summoned from prayer or teaching to manual work, neither for the same reason are we summoned to partake food? For I argue from a similar point, namely, that if he was not summoned to manual work for his duties of care as a bishop, therefore, for the same reason neither was he summoned to partake of food. And, certainly, it is evident that this argument is ridiculous, because our manual work is not as necessary for sustaining life as is food.[76]

The key here is Olivi's recognition that work is not as necessary to their life as food is. Could we have heard a similar statement from Francis? One last example on the following paragraph deals with the question of whether "it is better to work than not to work."[77] Olivi immediately points out that it depends on which kind of work we are comparing; for example, if we are comparing manual work with a work of higher quality, then certainly it is better not to work because we have the possibility then to join in a higher venture. Going

---

75 Ibid., 70.

76 Ibid., 71. Please note that in the original Latin the word used is *potestas*, which has a much broader meaning than the English *power*.

77 Ibid., 71.

into detail he explains: "Otherwise, it would have been more perfect for Paul to do manual work than it would have been for Christ not to work, which is not only false but in fact heretical." He certainly has a good answer for everything.

Concerning begging, in chapter 6, Olivi refutes one by one all the possible arguments against it, but the most intriguing is the lengthy discussion referring again to a question of power. It is the response to "certain adversaries" who, invoking Augustine, claim that "in Christ and the apostles the receiving of necessities was not mendicancy but power."[78] It shows that there were problems with an increasing hierarchical structure in the Order, and many were asking questions. Were the prelates supposed to receive what they needed without begging simply for their higher position? Was Christ provided with all necessities because he was received as a prelate or as a powerful overseer, or in any case as a man of power? Referring to many examples from the Scriptures, sometime with a tone obviously resentful of such questioning, Olivi eloquently demonstrates the contrary: "I would state that Christ or indeed an apostle, never used such power for themselves; because to the perfect and for the perfect it was not given for themselves, but only for providing more securely and easily for the need of the common good."[79] The fact that he spent quite a good number of pages trying to refute the question of the difference between a true beggar and the man of power illustrates for us the existence of new problems deriving from the friars' change in life style and from the different structure of the Order when compared to the beginning of the brotherhood at the time Francis was alive. Certainly we see a different dynamic in the friars' daily activities that does not correspond to our perception of Francis' vision.

We can conclude, however, that concerning the understanding of the Rule at this time, with all his exceptionally sophisticated learning, Olivi does not show a better understanding than others with less talent such as Hugh of Digne. To be honest, one could be suspicious of his ability to please friends and foes with the subtlety of his rhetoric. It is a fact that his adversaries could not find in all his writings anything for which they could accuse him; while at the same time he excited an enormous interest among the Spirituals who were against the official interpretation of the Rule and against the Franciscans' reinterpretation of Francis' *forma vitae*. Can we doubt his sincerity? Perhaps, he was just too clever.

In regard to his discussion on *usus pauper* there is no question that he wanted sincerely to find a way to integrate poverty in the friars' daily lives; but again, perhaps many of his brothers did not understand him as they had not understood Francis at his time. They wanted a rule that could spell out what to do for every minute of their day; the freedom of choice implicit in Olivi's

---
78 Ibid., 80.
79 Ibid., 86.

theory was not appreciated. There was too much responsibility attached, and the brothers needed instead the continuous protection of an iron rule that could tell them precisely what to do for the safety of their souls. Olivi's theoretical intervention in the late thirteenth century was not well received probably by a majority of brothers. His eloquence has great success today because finally his subtlety is taken into consideration and appreciated. We have to be careful not to take him as an example of his age; he looks more like a splendid exception to the uneventful life of many brothers who by now were set on the regular convent life of the Order, and were disturbed by the pretense of the Spirituals demanding a return to Franciscan purity.

What is really hard to understand is how it happened that Olivi became a symbol for the Spirituals. Supposedly he was keen on promoting the true Franciscan spirit. From our reading of his commentary on the Rule it does not seem to be a reality. If Olivi could have looked at work as an important factor, central to the economy of a balanced community life, his *usus pauper* would have made more sense; it could have been closer to Francis' pragmatic view of a spiritual life. It is true that, considering the mentality of the time, he would have attracted more negative reactions from his enemies, thus accelerating the pace of his persecution. On the other hand, he was perfectly in tune with his social environment. He did not want to deal with the work issue, not because he was afraid of his enemies: he simply could not, because his mentality of learned scholar had brought him far away from the idea of work, wrongly interpreted as a manual activity, as labor. His exceptional acumen did not help him to understand the organic action of work and *paupertas* on the life of a community conceived by Francis' pragmatic mind. His refined intellectualism took him on a hyperbolic reasoning far away from Francis' true *forma vitae*. We are fascinated by Olivi's ability to construct an imaginary castle in which everything has its right place. His flexibility finds a reason for everything and an excuse for all possible circumstances of life. His system worked for all involved parties in the *usus pauper* controversy. The Spirituals thought Olivi was defending them, while in fact he was following Bonaventure's ecstatic vision and the Four Masters' practical view of the Order's organization. The people in charge of the commission inquiring on his work's orthodoxy could not censure him because they were confronted by the subtlety of his reasoning capable of giving to each what they wanted. They had to await his death to accuse and condemn him. They had to wait for his voice to be silent, for him to be unable to defend his work.

The effort to understand Olivi's influence within the Franciscan environment cannot be complete without at least a brief look into the reality of the movement of the Spirituals. Angelo Clareno was a well-known personality among Spirituals, and he was an admirer of Olivi. Angelo Clareno also wrote his Commentary on the Rule; thus it will be perhaps possible to have a clear idea of the contact points between Olivi's and Clareno's approach to work.

WORK IN ANGELO CLARENO'S COMMENTARY ON THE RULE

Angelo Clareno is known among modern commentators as the main representative of the Spirituals. We will not deal with the history of the movement or with Clareno's eventful life, which have been already amply discussed by scholars.[80] For our purpose we focus exclusively on the text of his *Expositio super regulam Fratrum Minorem*, written between 1321 and 1323.[81] By then Olivi had already died, leaving behind the fame of his knowledge and sanctity.[82] Angelo Clareno refers very often to Olivi in his writing. By comparing Clareno's commentary to Olivi's, we may understand whether the Spirituals' approach to work could have been indeed a return to Francis' *forma vitae*. Looking briefly at the *Proemio*, we notice how forcefully Clareno insists upon Francis having "received the Rule and the interpretation directly from Christ, in accordance with the life of Christ, his Mother, the apostles and all the saints before him."[83] There were discussions at the time about this particular issue; we can imagine that the Order, as well as the papacy, was not keen on accepting the Rule as a revelation from God. It would have meant that they had to abide by everything stated in the Rule and this was not acceptable to them: only the Scriptures could be considered as coming directly through divine inspiration.

The first thing we notice is that, despite Clareno's assertion of wanting to go back to the original intent of Francis' *forma vitae*, he chose to comment on the Later Rule as Olivi does. This may demonstrate that he was not aware of any change or adjustment operated in the text since the drafting of the Early Rule. This would be, however, a wrong assumption because he shows instead a clear awareness at least on one particular issue that must have been of primary importance. In fact, in chapter 10 Clareno specifically insists on quoting directly from the Early Rule.[84] He is very carefully pointing out the difference in the requirement for "obedience" as explained in the Early and in the Later Rule. He contrasts the Early Rule with the Later Rule, claiming that

---

80 See David Burr, *The Spiritual Franciscans* (University Park: Pennsylvania State University Press, 2001).

81 *Expositio super regulam Fratrum Minorum di Frate Angelo Clareno* a cura di F. Giovanni Boccali (Edizioni Porziuncuoa: Assisi, 1994). Felice Accrocca wrote the introduction. The Latin text is translated in Italian by Marino Bigaroni.

82 Olivi's fame as a saint developed in Southern France among the Spiritual beguines. The Italian Spirituals did not have the same connotation. See David Burr's *The Spiritual Franciscans*.

83 Ibid.: « […] egli ricevette la Regola e la sua interpretazione direttamente da Cristo e che pienamente e perfettamente concorda, per il comportamento e gli esempi, alla vita di Cristo e della sua Madre, degli apostoli e di tutti i santi perfetti, che lo hanno preceduto […], 113. »

84 Ibid., 647.

the Early Rule contains Francis' true intent. In fact Francis stated at first in the Early Rule that the brothers were not bound to obedience when requested to do something against their conscience. He also stressed that to do something against their soul would not have meant to be in obedience but to commit a crime. The same notion was formulated in a milder tone in the Later Rule: the brothers must be obedient to their superiors in everything they promised unless requested to do something contrary to their soul and to the Rule. The second statement is clearly more on the side of the Order's hierarchic system. Clareno insists on considering Francis' statements in the Early Rule as more in tune with his original intent. Olivi had also spoken at length about obedience, affirming that the friars were not supposed to obey a command that contradicted their commitment to the Rule: actually, even more strongly, the friar had the responsibility to disobey superiors if they demanded violation of the Rule.[85] This was very much at the heart of Olivi's argument and constituted also the point of contact with the Spirituals' credo: it was a major cause of disturbance for the Order's leadership and certainly a central one that caused the persecution of the Spirituals. In any case Clareno shows his preoccupation about the issue of obedience by quoting the Early Rule, posing it as Francis' real intent; thus he was perfectly conscious that between the Early and the Later Rule there was a difference in the quality of life described by Francis. Why did he not exercise the same awareness when dealing with the work issue?

Clareno's insistence in the *Proemio* that Francis had received the Rule by divine inspiration,[86] together with his preoccupation on making clear the meaning of Franciscan obedience were two basic tenets for the Spirituals and constituted a problem for the papacy. For the Spirituals, the comment to the Rule was essential; it clarified Francis' intention, his commitment to follow the Gospel in a daily life centered on a Christ-like experience. The commentary on the Rule became then the base upon which the Spirituals meant to interpret and participate in Francis' *forma vitae*. Felice Accrocca notes the importance taken by the commentaries on the Rule at a time in which the papacy was emitting new limitations to the Rule's interpretation.[87] Moreover, at the same time the issue of poverty was gaining intensity with the *usus pauper* contro-

---

85 Olivi's *Commentary on the Rule*, 105, B2: "[...] they are to be obedient in all things they have promised (not to human beings, but rather to God and in all things that are not contrary to the soul or Rule)." He reminds the reader that he has already explained the issue in the question on evangelical obedience.

86 In the Italian translation: *da Cristo*.

87 Felice Accrocca, *Expositio super regulam Fratrum Minorum di Frate Angelo Clareno:* "Per reagire ai cambiamenti introdotti nella vita dell'Ordine dagli interventi papali operati sulla Regola, gli Spirituali fecero riferimento alla « intentio prima et ultima" di Francesco e alla sua intima e privilegiata esperienza interiore. ... Non è un caso ... che proprio nel loro ambiente i problemi relativi alla Regola furono percepiti con tale sensibilità da dare origine a ben tre commenti (49-50)." He refers to the three major commentaries we are examining, the commentary on the Rule by Hugh of Digne, Peter of John Olivi and Angelo Clareno. He adds also the *Articuli accepti de Regula* by Ubertino da Casale written during the polemic during the Council of Vienne.

versy. As we already gathered from previous examples in Hugh and Olivi's commentaries if we ask the reason why Clareno did not exercise the same awareness for the work issue as he did for obedience, the answer may be quite simple. The issue of work had ceased to exist. Despite the claim of wanting to respect Francis' intention, the Spirituals were blind to the necessity of including work as Francis had requested in the Early Rule. This is strange indeed if we consider Clareno's clear understanding expressed in his own statement on the obedience issue. Supposedly the brothers had to profess what was written in the Rule, insisting that it had to be in the *First Rule*: "...nichil eis precipientes, quod siit contra animam suam et regulam promissam, *in prima regula*..."[88]

Instead, in chapter 5 of his commentary, *de modo laborandi*, Clareno is not in tune with the spirit of the Early Rule; "*gratiam laborandi*" the grace of work has the ultimate purpose of fighting the tendency to idleness, which is the "enemy of the soul," as stated in the Later Rule. Clareno also quotes the *Testament* that for him existed in an indivisible reality with the Rule. For the Spirituals the *Testament* complemented, with Francis' last words, everything already established in the Rule. However, we discover some ambiguity in the *Testament* where we read: "Let those who do not know how to work learn, not from desire to receive wages, but for example and to avoid idleness."[89] In the *Testament*, as in the Later Rule, there is no mention of the original description of working fully explained in the Early Rule. Is the *Testament* totally faithful to Francis' last wishes?

Hagiography tells us that Francis was very ill and could not see: his brothers helped him with writing. Is it possible that the text may have been influenced by the interpretation of the brothers who wrote it under Francis' dictation or copied it right after his death? We find a similar suggestion in a note to the English translation of the *Testament*, concerning the perceived change in the tone of the text.[90] The note refers specifically to Francis, who is apparently accepting the change to the *forma vitae* already implemented by the brothers. It is suggested that Francis' submission to it represents a renunciation to his previous conviction: "recognizing the gradual development of accepting churches and residences, a step away from his original view of poverty...."[91] It can be argued that we have a similar occurrence in the work issue, considering that the *forma vitae* had already undergone a significant modification from the

---

88 Ibid., 644, chaper 10: "... non comandando loro nulla che sia contrario alla loro anima o alla Regola professata, nella *Regola prima*... »

89 *Francis of Assisi; Early Documents*, 125.

90 Ibid.,126 a : "The Testament takes a decidedly different direction at this point as Francis ceases to reminisce about the early days of his life and those of his brothers and begins a series of exhortations and commands. This change has led some to conclude that the document was written at different times and, perhaps, with the assistance of different brothers who took his dictation."

91 Ibid., 126.

Early to the Later Rule. The *Testament* must have become also involved in the same process.

It follows that even with the help given by the *Testament,* Clareno could not have any remembrance of Francis' true vision for his community in regard to *ars*, which is important for the understanding of Francis' original approach to work in the Early Rule. Clareno quotes from the Early Rule, but he does not seem to have a complete perception of Francis' intent, even though he claims to care so much about it. Again Accrocca, in the introduction to the commentary, writes that whenever the brothers asked Clareno to clarify Francis' true intention, he would invite them to go back to the original Francis and to the experience of the first brotherhood, because only then it would have been possible to perceive what Francis really wanted for himself and his companions.[92] Given the mood of the time, it is not surprising that Clareno could not completely follow his own encouragement. In the next passage, quoting this time from the *Compilatio Assisiensis,* among other documents, Clareno explains that, besides the obligation to preach, the brothers must continuously pray, go begging and work with their hands; quoting again from the *Testament,* he reports Francis' words "*Ego manibus meis laboravi*" (I worked with my hands).[93]

As for Olivi, Clareno's conception regards work as labor, and its main purpose is keeping the friars busy avoiding idleness. Clareno strengthens the idea of fighting idleness with work using eloquent descriptions of what might happen to the brothers who do not follow "faithfully and devoutly" Francis' admonition. At this point he quotes from the Early Rule precisely the important passage in which Francis explains *de modo laborandi*. While we expect some kind of acknowledgement about the nature of the work described by Francis, Clareno simply reports the passage as if it were self-explanatory of what he had just said in regard to the importance of fighting idleness. He does not add any other comment, but his following passage does enough to explain his thinking. He goes on to describe how St. Basil clearly taught the necessity of praying and giving thanks to God without neglecting work. According to St. Basil, the brothers must work in order to have enough to give to the poorest. Thus, they must commit to work in any kind of circumstance, even though working can be at the time unbearably hard: suffering through work is not only advantageous as a punishment for the body, but also as charity for others.[94]

---

92 Ibid., 83 : « Ai compagni che gli chiedevano con insistenza chiarificazioni *sulla vera intentio* di Francesco, il Clareno risponde, dunque, con l'invito a tornare a Francesco stesso e all'esperienza della primitiva fraternitas : solo in quella dimensione si può percepire con autenticità cosa, in realtà, Francesco volle per sè e per i suoi. »

93 Ibid., 397; 5, 9-11.

94 *Expositio super regulam Fratrum Minorum di Frate Angelo Clareno*, 404-405 : « ... Nel lavoro, nei travagli, nelle vigilie oltre il giusto, nella fame e nella sete. Questa tale istituzione è proficua per noi non solo come castigo del corpo, ma anche a scopo di carità verso il prossimo. »

Whoever works in this manner is able to avoid idleness without extinguishing the need for praying and devotion. After St. Basil, Clareno brings the example of St. Jerome, who wrote about St. John the hermit taking only Eucharist on Sunday as nourishment for his body and thus being blessed by God with many spiritual gifts: nevertheless he did not neglect working with his hands, and while fasting he used to make straps for mules. The next example is St. Paul of Thebe, who worked with his hands using the leaves and the fruits from the palm trees for food and clothing. Once a year, St. Paul offered his crafts to God by burning them. Clareno ends the chapter on work by mentioning those hermits who, after selling their handcrafts in Egypt, did not keep anything for themselves, but rather, they gave all the gain from their work to the poorest and the sick. St. Basil, St. Jerome, St. John the hermit, St. Paul of Thebe and all the old hermits are overwhelmingly more significant than Francis; or rather, Francis is modeled upon their example.

There is not much more on *paupertas* that could be interesting for our purpose. He practically repeats what he has just said concerning the eremitical life style; the hermits did not accept money, used their manual work for the benefits of others and lived on the fruit and leaves of trees: theirs was extreme poverty. Clareno honors the memory of the first Fathers who lived in conformity with the life of Christ. He definitely stresses the necessity of a life in imitation of Christ as the ideal of the true Franciscan *forma vitae*. However, even though the idea of donating to the poorest the fruit of their labor is in harmony with Francis' intention, the fact of living in the harsh conditions of extreme poverty and being prone to severe ascetical practices was not a part of the *forma vitae*. Just like Hugh and Olivi, Clareno has come a long way farther from the Francis of the Early Rule.

In his *Epilogus* for Peter of John Olivi, Clareno proclaims his admiration for him. He regrets Olivi had been mistreated by his enemies and also by his brothers. It would seem that Clareno's esteem for Olivi was due to an exceptional personality misunderstood by many, as often happens with great men or women throughout history. Assuming that Angelo Clareno can be really considered a representative for the Spirituals, the only points of contact with Olivi are the issue of obedience and the desire of respecting Francis' intent. However, both Olivi and Clareno refer to an image of Francis that at their time had been already codified and internalized by a majority; it had lost the human touch of a real personality, working in this world, participating actively in the life of the surrounding society. As it happened to Hugh, in their heart they struggled with a feeling of nostalgia for something lost, something more than a disincarnated entity. They were destined to be unfulfilled. Or perhaps they knew more than it could be said.

Conclusion

The result of our brief reading of Hugh of Digne, Peter of John Olivi and Angelo Clareno is the image of a romanticized and spiritualized Francis in stark contrast with the pragmatic Francis found in the Early Rule. It is the Francis suggested by Celano, codified by the papacy and blessed by Bonaventure, who finally identified Francis with the apocalyptic Angel of the Sixth Seal. Already in Hugh's time, about thirty years after Francis' death, work and *paupertas* are completely separate issues. Why? I imagine people were not ready for Francis' innovative concept. There were misunderstandings, false interpretations and finally the projection of traditional forms of devotion into the new society proposed by Francis. *Paupertas* became the greatest concern because, once isolated from real life, it lost its value and could not exist without mutating into the old ascetic poverty, changing its original quality and purpose. Work, instead of having the essential place it deserved in a growing community, acquired the typical monastic shape, which in the friars' everyday life alternated with the duty of preaching and doing "spiritual things." Work, in fact, became mostly an expedient for avoiding the temptation that accompanies idleness, while poverty was the harsh, material poverty that tortures the body for the exaltation of the spirit.

Hugh, Olivi and Clareno all claimed a return to Francis' purity of intent, and they all failed to consider the work issue as the key to living in *paupertas*. As we said at the beginning of this paper, Francis chose to live among the *minores* in society, and it was precisely from *minoritas* that *paupertas* derived. His commitment to material poverty did not mean that friars did not have everything needed for their existence; also it did not mean that they had to torture their bodies with the excessive rigor of fasting. Clareno and Olivi refer with admiration to monastic life, in which the concept of living and working among the *minores* was nonexistent. Their vision of the Franciscan Order was not different from the official vision: a life in a convent with a compelling duty to preach while taking care of the lay community that by now was not included within the Franciscan experience as it was advocated by Francis.

The Franciscan Order became a great institution under the impulse given by the papacy, regardless of having acquired a shape of its own with no resemblance to its founder. But we can imagine a possible Francis as defined by the *propositum vitae* of 1209, the first stage of the Early Rule, when Francis' intent was still untouched by doubt and suspicion: pragmatic, with a realistic and constructive view of society, far-sighted in his refusal of using money, embracing diversity, promoting peace, but also fighting for truth, living with joy and love. Whoever he was, Francis was real and his *forma vitae* was a fleeting moment of pure beauty lost in the mediocrity of human history.

BIBLIOGRAPHY

Primary Sources

Battista, Hyeronima. Pesaro: Biblioteca Oliveriana, 454, II (XVII - XVIII centuries), ff.44r-45v.
Clareno, Angelo. *Expositio Super Regulam Fratrum Minorem*. Ed. Giovanni Boccali. Assisi, Chiesa Nuova: Biblioteca Francescana, Edizioni Porziuncola, 1994.
Dante, Alighieri. *Paradiso* · Canto XXXI v.1-29.
Francis of Assisi : Early Documents, The Saint. Vol. I Eds. Regis J. Armstrong, J. A.Wayne Hellmann and William Short. New York: New City Press, 1999.
Hugh of Dignes's Rule Commentary. Ed. David Flood. Grottaferrata: Collegii S. Bonaventurae ad Claras Aqua, 1979.
———. *Commentary on the Rule of the Lesser Brothers by Hugh of Digne*. Introduction by David Flood. To be published by the Franciscan Institute.
Olivi, Petrus Ioannis. *De Usu Paupere. De Quaestio and the Tractatus*. Ed. David Burr. University of Western Australia, Perth: Leo Olschki Editore, 1992.
———. *Commentary on the Rule of the Lesser Brothers by Peter of John Olivi*. Ed. David Flood. To be published by the Franciscan Institute.
Rolandino. *Cronaca; vita e morte di Ezzelino Romano*. Ed. Flavio Forese. Fondazione Lorenzo Valla: Arnoldo Mondadori Editore, 2005.

Secondary Sources

Arnaldi, Girolamo. "Il mito di Ezzelino da Rolandino a Mussato," *La cultura*, 18, 1980; 155-165.
Baxandall, Michael. *Giotto and the Orators*. Oxford: Clarendon Press, 1971.
Bell, Rudolph. *Holy Anorexia*. Chicago and London: University of Chicago Press, 1985.
Boccali, Giovanni. *Textus Opusculorum S.Francisci et S.Clarae Assisensium*. Assisi: Ed. Portiuncula, (1976).

———. "Leggenda in rima su S.Chiara d'Assisi." *Frate Francesco, 71* (2005): 389-414.
Burr, David. *The Persecution of Peter Olivi*. Philadelphia: The American Philosophical Society, 1976.
———. *Olivi and Franciscan Poverty*. Philadelphia: University of Pennsylvania, 1989.
———. *The Spiritual Franciscans*. Philadelphia: University of Pennsylvania, 2001.
Cacciotti, Alvaro and Maria Melli. Eds. *La grazia del lavoro*. Milan: Biblioteca Francescana, 2010.
Camporesi, Piero. « Cultura popolare e cultura d'élite fra Medioevo ed età moderna.» *Storia d'Italia. Intellettuali e potere*. Annali 4. Turin: Einaudi (1981), 81-58.
Canonici, Luciano. *Santa Lucia di Foligno. Storia di un monastero e di un ideale*. S. Maria degli Angeli: Edizioni Portiuncola, 1974.
Caroli, Ernesto. "Biografie di San Francesco. I Fioretti; Considerazioni sulle Stimmate" *Fonti Francescane*. Padova: Editrici Francescane (2004):1234.
Carraro, Giannino. "Il monachesimo padovano durante la dominazione ezzeliniana" (1237-1256). *Nuovi Studi Ezzeliniani*. Ed. Giorgio Gracco. Roma: Palazzo Borromini, 1992.
Crawford, Galea Kate. "Unhappy Choices: Factors that Contributed to the Decline and Condemnation of the Beguines" *On Pilgrimage, The Best of Vox Benedictina 1984-1993*. Winnipeg, Manitoba: Hignell Printing, 1994.
Cusato, Michael. "Whence the Community?" *Franciscan Study* 60 (2002), 39-80.
———. "Poverty and Prosperity: Franciscans and the Use of Money." Ed. Daria Mitchell *Washington Theological Union* Symposium Papers (2009).
Dalarun, Jacques and Fabio Zinelli. "Le manuscrit des sœurs de Santa Lucia de Foligno 1 Notice" *Studi medievali*, 46 (2005): 117-167.
———. "Poésie et théologie à Santa Lucia de Foligno. Sur une laude de Battista de Montefeltro." *Caterina Vigri. La santa e la città*. Atti del Convegno Bologna, 13-15 Nov. (2002):19-43.
Flood, David. "The Theology of Peter John Olivi" *The History of Franciscan Theology*. Ed. Kenan Obsborne. St. Bonaventure, New York: The Franciscan Institute (2007), 127-184.
———. *Francis of Assisi and the Franciscan Movement*. Quezon City, Philippines: FIA Contact Publication, 1989.
———. *The Daily Labor of the Early Franciscans*. St. Bonaventure, New York: The Franciscan Institute Publications, 2010.
———. *Work for Every One. Francis of Assisi and the Ethic of Service*. Inter Franciscan Center Quezon City, Philippines: CCFMC Office for Asia/Oceania, 1997.
———. "Peace in Assisi in the Thirteenth Century," *Franziskanische Studien*, 68-80.
———. *La nascita di un carisma*. Milano : Biblioteca Francescana Provinciale, 1976.
———. *The Persecution of Peter Olivi*. Philadelphia: The American Philosophical Society, 1976.
———. *Olivi and Franciscan Poverty*. Philadelphia: University of Pennsylvania, 1989.
Galloway, Penny. "Neither Miraculous Nor Astonishing. The Devotional Practice of Beguine Communities in French Flanders." *New Trends in Feminine Spirituality*. Ed. Juliette Dor, Lesley Johnson and Joceline Wogan-Browne. Centre for Medieval Studies University of Hull: Brepols, 1999.
Gamboso, Vergilio. *Vita prima di Sant'Antonio o Assidua*. Padua : Edizioni Messaggero,1984.
———. *Antonio di Padova.Vita e spiritualità*. Padua: Edizioni Messaggero, 1995.
Ginzburg, Carlo. "Folklore, magia, religione." *Storia d'Italia. I caratteri originali II*. Torino: Einaudi tascabili (1989): 603-678.
Klenberg, Aviad. "Canonization without a Canon." *Procès de canonization au Moyen Âge; aspects juridiques et religieux*. École française de Rome, 2004; 7-18.
Lambert, Malcolm. *The Cathars*. Oxford and Malden, MA: Blakewell Publishing, 1998, 2007.

―――. *Medieval Heresy. Popular Movements from the Gregorian Reform to the Reformation.* Oxford and Malden, MA: Blackwell Publishing, 2002.

Little, Lester K. *Evangelical Poverty, the New Money Economy and Violence. Poverty in the Middle Ages.* Ed. David Flood. Franziskanische Forschungen 27. Dietrich-Celde-Verlag, Werl/Westf (1975):11-26.

―――. *Religious Poverty and the Profit Economy in Medieval Europe.* Ithaca, NewYork: Cornell University Press, 1978, 1983.

Manselli, Raoul. *St. Francis of Assisi.* Chicago: Franciscan Herald Press, 1988.

―――. "Ezzelino da Romano, Nella politica italiana del sec. XIII." *Studi Ezzeliniani,* Vols. 45-47. Roma: Palazzo Borromini, 1963; 35-79.

―――. "San Francesco e l'eresia." *Annali della Facoltà di Lettere e Filosofia.* Università di Siena, 5. 1984; 51-70.

―――. "Padova e S. Antonio." *Studi per la Storia del Santo a Padova,* III. Ed. A. Popp. Venice: Neri Pozza, 1976; 3-14.

Marangon, Paolo. *Alle origini dell'aristotelismo padovano (sec. XII-XIII).* Padova: Editrice Antenore, 1977.

Mariani, Eliodoro. *I fioretti di San Francesco. Considerazioni sulle stimmate.* Vicenza: Dolo, 1977.

Meersseman, Gilles Gerard. *Ordo Fraternitatis, Confraternite e pietà dei laici nel medioevo.* Roma: Herder Editrice, 1977.

Merlo, Grado. "La santità di Antonio e il problema degli eretici." *Il Santo,* 36 Centro Studi Antoniani: Università di Padova, 1996.

―――. "Storia di frate Francesco e dell'Ordine dei Minori." *Francesco d'Assisi e il primo secolo di storia francescana.* Turin: Einaudi, 1997.

Miccoli, Giovanni. "La storia religiosa." *Storia d'Italia. Dalla caduta dell'Impero Romano al secolo XVIII.* Volume secondo. Giulio Einaudi Editore: Torino, 1974; 431- 1071.

Monti, Dominic. *Francis and His Brothers: A Popular History of the Franciscan Friars.* Cincinnati, Ohio: St. Anthony Messenger Press, 2008.

Moorman, John. *A History of the Franciscan Order. From Its Origin to the Year 1517.* Chicago: Franciscan Herald Press, 1988.

Newman, Barbara. "Possessed by the Spirit: Devout Women, Demoniacs, and the Apostolic Life in the Thirteenth Century." *Speculum,* 73, No. 3 (July 1998): 733-770.

Nicolini, Ugo. "Stefano Guarnieri da Osimo, cancelliere di Perugia dal 1466 al 1488." *L'Umanesimo Umbro, Atti del IX Convegno di Studi Umbri.* Gubbio (1974): 324-329.

Paciocco, Roberto. "Nondum post mortem beati Antonii annus effluxerat. La santità romano-apostolica di Antonio e l'esemplarità di Padova nel contesto dei coevi processi di canonizzazione" *Il Santo,* 36. Centro Studi Antoniani: Università di Padova, 1996.

Papi, Anna Benvenuti. *In castro poenitentiae. Santità e società femminile nell'Italia medievale.* Roma : Herder Editrice, 1990.

Pellegrini, Luigi. « Fratres qui stant apud alios ad serviendum vel laborandum » *La grazia del lavoro,* Ed. Alvaro Cacciotti and Maria Melli. Milano: Biblioteca Francescana (2010); 37- 57.

Pini, Antonio Ivan. « Le arti in processione. Professioni, prestigio e potere nelle città-stato dell'Italia padana medievale » *Lavorare nel medioevo : rappresentazioni ed esempi dall'Italia dei secc. X-XVI,* 12-15 ottobre 1980 Convegni del centro di studi sulla spiritualità medievale. Università degli studi di Perugia XXI. Todi (1983): 67-107.

Piron, Sylvain et Alain Boureau. Ed. *Pierre De Jean Olivi (1248-1298) Pensée Scolastique, Dissidence Spirituelle et Société.* Paris: Librairie Philosophique J.Vrin, 1999.

———. "Perfection Évangélique et Moralité Civile: Pierre de Jean Olivi et l'Étique Économique Franciscaine." *In Ideologia del Credito fra Tre e Quattrocento: Dall'Astesiano ad Angelo da Chivasso.* Eds. Barbara Molina and Giulia Scarcia. Collana del Centro Studi sui Lombardi e sul Credito nel Medioevo, 3 Asti (2001):102-43.

———. "Le Poète et le Théologien: Une Rencontre dans le Studium de Santa Croce." *Picenum Seraphicum* 19 (2000): 87-134.

Polizzi, Carlo. *Studi e documenti Ezzeliniani. Ezzelino da Romano. Signoria territoriale e comune cittadino.* Comune di Romano D'Ezzelino, Sezione Cultura e Ricerca Storica, 1989.

Rigon, Antonio. "Religione e politica al tempo dei da Romano. Giordano Forzatè e la tradizione agiografica antiezzeliniana." *Nuovi Studi Ezzeliniani.* Ed. Giorgio Gracco. Roma: Palazzo Borromini, 1992.

———. S. Antonio da "Pater Padue" a "Patronus Civitatis." *Francesco d'Assisi e gli Ordini mendicanti.* Edizioni Porziuncola, 2005; 65-76.

———. *Dal libro alla folla. Antonio di Padova e il francescanesimo nedievale.* Roma: Viella, 2002

———. "Attorno a Sant'Antonio di Padova, Conclusioni a Vite e vita di Antonio di Padova." *Atti del convegno internazionale sulla agiografia antoniana.* Padova, 29 maggio -1 giugno 1995.

———. *The Laity in the Middle Ages. Religious Beliefs and Devotional Practices.* Ed. Daniel Bornstein. Trans. Margery Schneider. Notre Dame, IN, and London: University of Notre Dame Press, 1993.

———. *Ordini mendicanti e società italiana, XIII-XV secolo.* Il Saggiatore: Milano, 1990.

Schlager, Bernard. "Foundresses of the Franciscan Life." *Viator,* 29. (1988): 141-166.

Simons, Walter. *Cities of Ladies.* Philadelphia: University of Pennsylvania Press, 2001.

Thompson, Augustine. *Revival Preachers and Politics in Thirteenth-century Italy. The Great Devotion of 1233.* Oxford: Clarendon Press,1992.

———. *Cities of God. The Religion of the Italia Communes 1125-1325.* State College, PA: Penn State University Press, 2005.

Todeschini, Giacomo. *Franciscan Wealth. From Voluntary Poverty to Market Society,* Trans. Donatella Melucci. New York: The Franciscan Institute Publications, 2009.

———. *I mercanti e il tempio. La società cristiana e il circolo virtuoso della ricchezza fra Medioevo ed Età Moderna.* Bologna : Il Mulino, 2002.

———. *Visibilmente crudeli. Malviventi, persone sospette e gente qualunque dal Medioevo all'età moderna.* Bologna : Il Mulino, Saggi, 2007.

———. *Economie urbane ed etica economica nell'Italia Medievale.* Ed. R.Greci e G. Pinto. Rome: Laterza, 2005.

———. "Oeconomica Francescana II: Pietro di Giovanni Olivi come fronte per la Storia dell'Etica-Economica Medievale," *Rivista di Storia e Letteratura Religiosa,* 13 (1977): 461-494.

Troncelliti, Latifah. "All'ombra della Controriforma. Dal *Discorso* di Paleotti alla *Ricotta* di Pasolini." *Italica. Journal of the American Association of Teachers of Italian,* 84. No.2-3 (Summer/Autumn 2007): 548-555.

Vauchez, André. *The Laity in the Middle Ages. Religious Beliefs and Practices.* Ed. Daniel Bornstein, Trans. Margery Schneider. Notre Dame, IN, and London: University of Notre Dame Press, 1987.

———. "Alle origini del processo di canonizzazione" *Diventare santo; itinerari e riconoscimenti della santità tra libri, documenti e immagini.* Eds. G. Morello, A. Piazzoni, P. Vian. Biblioteca Apostolica Vaticana: Events, 1998.

———. *La sainteté en occident aux derniers siécles du moyen age.* École française de Rome, Palais Farnese, 1981.

———. *Sainthood in the Later Middle Ages.* Trans. Jean Birrel. Cambridge and New York: Cambridge University Press,1997.

Zarri, Gabriella. «Monasteri femminili e città.» *Storia d'Italia. La chiesa e il potere politico.* Annali v. 9. Torino: Einaudi Editore (1986): 359-429, 361-363.

Zumthor, Paul. *La mesure du monde. Représentation de l'espace au Moyen Age.* Paris: Edition du Seuil, 1993.

INDEX

Accrocca, Felice, 110, 112
Actus/Fioretti, 30
agents, 90–91, 103
Agostino da Stroncone, 59
À la recherche du temps perdu (Proust), 5
Alexander IV, 31
allegory, *Sacrum Commercium* as, 52–53
Alleluia movement, 26, 38
alms, 87, 90, 93, 95–96, 103, 105, 107
Angelo, 7
animals, and Francis, 13
Anthony, 90
    attitude of toward sainthood, 28
    canonization of, 20–24, 27
    and interpretation of Franciscan rule, 23
    lack of interest in heresy, 29–30
    spirituality of, image of, 31
Antonia, 63
"*ars*", 80, 81, 84, 85, 90, 112
    See also work
Arsenio da Montepulciano, 47
asceticism, 11
    See also fasting
Assidua, 20–21, 29–30
Assisi, 77
Assisi Compilation, 6–15
St. Augustine, 105, 106, 107

Authié, Jacques, 55

baptistery, centrality of, 39
St. Basil, 112–13
basilica
    construction of, 86
    Francis's rejection of, 57
begging, 87, 90, 93, 95–96, 103, 105, 107
beguines
    declared heretics, 49, 62
    Pope's view of, 37
    religiosity of, 72
    transformation of, 65
    See also lay communities, women's
Bell, R., 44, 47
Benignitas, 30
Bevegnati, Giunta, 45, 49
Bianco, Frank, 2
Bigaroni, Marino, 7
Boccaferro, Giovanni, 64, 65
Boccali, Giovanni, 63, 67
Bonaventure, 97, 108
Boniface VIII, 100
bread, blessed, 14–15
Brook, Rosalind, 7
Brufani, Stefano, 52
Bruni Aretino, Leonardo, 66
Burr, David, 98, 99, 100, 101

Caesar of Speyer, 54
Campeggi, Giovanni, 64
canonization
    of Anthony, 20–24, 27
    of Clare, 23
    and control, 19–20
    of Dominic, 20, 22, 23
    of Francis, 23
    power of, 28–32
    process of, 17–32
    requirements for, 18
    See also sainthood
Cantico delle creature (Francis), 13
Casali (family), 45
Cathars, 14–15, 42, 43, 55, 56
Cattani, Pietro, 11, 84
Celano's Second Life of Francis, 7
ceremony of the blessed bread, 14–15
chastity, 42–43
Chiara. *See* Clare
Chronica XXIV generalium, 28
Church, Catholic
    authority of, *vs.* civil, 59, 61
    influence of, 36
    need of for support, 20
cities, 34, 38–40, 41
Cities of God (Thompson), 34
civil authority, *vs.* Church authority, 59, 61
Clare
    canonization of, 23
    Legenda of Santa Chiara, 67, 68–70
    representation of spirituality of, 45
Clareno, Angelo, 108–13, 114
Clement V, 6, 37, 49, 62
coins, 102
    See also money
commercial revolution, 53, 54
    See also economy
communes
    establishment of lay communities in, 41
    See also cities
consciousness, 5–6
Constantine the Great, 55, 56
control, 47
convents
    economic structure of, 66
    intellectual activity in, 71, 72
    lay communities transformed into, 62
    life in, 64, 65

Monteluce, 50, 72
motivations for entering, 65–66
need for, 64–65
and religious belief, 63–64
Santa Chiara, 61–62
scholarship in, 65–72
and wealth, 66, 71
See also monasteries; Santa Lucia, Monastery of
corporality, 91–92
Corrado, Giacomo, 21
Cortona, 45, 46
Così è se vi pare (Pirandello), 5
creatures, and Francis, 13
Crusades, 40, 45
Cum dicat Dominus (Gregory IX), 24
Cum secundum evangelicam veritatem (Innocent III), 19
Cunegunda, 19
Cusato, Michael, 2, 52, 57, 74

Dalarun, Jacques, 9, 12, 13, 66, 67, 71
Dante Alighieri, 67–68
Decretales Gregorii IX, 19
Delorme, Ferdinand, 6, 7
Delphine of Puimichel, 42–43
demons, Church's need for, 40–41
Discretion, 57
disobedience, 100
documents, written, 33–34
Dominic, 20, 22, 23
dualism, 13–14
Duvernoy, Jean, 55

Early Rule
    begging in, 95–96
    in Clareno's commentary, 109–10, 112
    lifestyle in, 79
    Olivi on, 104
    simplicity of, 89
    work in, 74, 82, 88
    See also Rule of St. Francis
economy
    Francis's rejection of, 77
    money in, 83
    and poverty, 101–2
    religion's connection with, 34
education
    Francis's attitude toward, 90

university, 89–90
  of women, 70–71
Einstein, Albert, 5
Elias, 10
Elzéar, 42–43
Exempla (Jacques de Vitry), 40–41
Exiit qui seminat (Nicholas III), 102, 104, 105
Expositio super regulam Fratrum Minorem (Angelo Clareno), 109–13
Ezzelino da Romano, 24, 25–28, 31, 39, 40

Faloci-Pulignani, Michele, 72
fasting, 44, 47, 48, 114
financial institutions, development of, 77
Flood, David, 52, 53, 77, 78, 79, 84, 88, 100–101
Foligno, 59
  See also Santa Lucia, Monastery of
food, 106
  See also fasting
Foresight, 57
forma vitae, Francis's
  debate over, 79
  desire to return to, 75, 109 (*See also* Spirituals)
  disappearance of work from, 54, 74, 102–3
  Flood on, 77
  Francis's submission to changes in, 111
  historical reality of, 76
  interpretations of, 76–79
  loss of, 114
  as reaction to social ills, 77
  relation with Church's expectations, 75
  transformation of, 53, 54, 86–87
  work in, 79–88
  See also poverty
Forzatè, Giordano, 21, 25
Four Masters, 91, 92, 95, 103, 108
Francesco da Barberino, 48–49
Franciscan Order
  adaptation of to social convenience, 93
  alienation of from work, 87 (*See also* work)
  betrayal of Francis's spirit by, 83
  Church's agenda for, 30, 53–54, 55, 86, 105
  confusion affecting, 88–89
  debate over *forma vitae* in, 79 (*See also forma vitae,* Francis's)
  desire for precise rule for, 107–8
  establishment of, 74
  hierarchic structure of, 106, 107, 110
  lack of faith in *forma vitae* in, 94
  official vision of, 114
  original ideal of, 1–2
  protected by Church, 105
  purpose of, 57
  return of to traditional convent life, 49, 91
  right of to existence, 88
  struggle within, 52
  tension in, 10
  used against heresy, 55
  use of by Church, 87
  women in, 56
  and women's associations, 49
  and work (*See* work)
  See also Fratres Minores
Franciscan Question, 6, 51
Francis of Assisi
  attitude of toward other people, 11–12
  attitude of toward sainthood, 28
  beginning of vocation, 76–77
  canonization of, 20
  Church's presentation of, 2
  environment of, 14
  identity of, 6
  image of, 9–14, 74, 75, 79, 113, 114
  lifestyle of, 11
  as myth, 97
  as pragmatic, 78, 114
  rejection of basilica, 57
  Rule of (*See* Rule of St. Francis)
  Testament (*See Testament,* Francis's)
  usefulness of to Church, 20
  way of life, 73 (*See also forma vitae,* Francis's; poverty)
  writings of, 51
  See also forma vitae, Francis's; Rule of St. Francis; *Testament,* Francis's
Francis of Assisi, Early Documents, 6
Fratres Minores
  original ideal of, 1–2, 20
  transformation of, 20, 21
  See also Franciscan Order
Frederick II, 22, 25, 27
freedom, 99–100

friend, spiritual, 90–91, 103

Ghibillines, 25, 45
Greed, 57
Gregorio Magno (Gregory I), 36
Gregory IX
   agenda of for Franciscan Order, 53, 54
   canonizations during pontificate of, 19–20, 22, 27
   construction of basilica, 57, 86
   Cum dicat Dominus, 24
   Decretales Gregorii IX, 19
   Mira circa nos, 24
   Nimis iniqua, 87
   Quo elongati, 21, 23, 52, 53, 74, 86–87, 94
   Quoniam abundavit, 87
   transformation of *forma vitae,* 53, 86–87
   transformation of Rule, 90 (*See also Quo elongati*)
   use of Franciscan Order, 1
   views of beguines, 37
   See also Hugolino; Ugolino
Gregory VII, 19
Grundman, Herbert, 34
Guarnieri, Caterina of Osimo, 62, 63, 65, 66, 67
Guarnieri (family), 64
Guelphs, 25–26

hagiographers, 45
heresy/heretics
   and Anthony, 29–30
   beguines, 49, 62
   Cathars, 14–15, 42, 43, 55, 56
   definition of, 55
   and devotional practices, 42–43
   Ezzelino da Romano, 24, 25–28, 31, 39, 40
   influence of, 42–43
   lack of interest in, 29
   and lay communities, 42, 64
   as papal problem, 29
   political motivations and, 28, 31
   and saints, 44
   use of Franciscan Order against, 55
hermits, 77, 113
history
   force of, 83–84
   making of, 85
Holy Anorexia (Bell), 44

Honorius III, 37, 79
Hugh of Digne, 88–97, 114
Hugolino, 10, 12
   See also Gregory IX; Ugolino
humility, 47, 48
Hyeronima Malatesta, 62, 65–71

identity, complexity of, 5–6
identity, Francis's, 6
   ambiguity of, 14
   as artificial construct, 12
   attempts to find, 8–15
   image of, 9–14, 74, 75, 79, 113, 114
idleness, 82, 104, 112, 114
Innocent III, 18, 19, 79
In Search of Lost Time (Proust), 5
Italy
   social environment of, 76
   See also cities; economy

Jacques de Vitry, 40–41
Jerome of Ascoli, 98
Jerusalem, 45
John of Murrovalle, 100
John of Vicenza, 26
John the hermit, 113
John XXII, 100
Jordan of Giano, 28

Klenberg, Aviad, 17–18, 31

labor, 81, 85, 90, 112
   See also work
La coscienza di Zeno (Svevo), 5
Lady Poverty, 52, 55, 56, 57, 73, 85
The Laity in the Middle Ages (Vauchez), 35
language
   changes in, 36
   in Rule, 80 (*See also* "ars")
Later Rule
   approval of, 79
   Clareno's commentary on, 109–13
   money in, 82
   work in, 82, 88
   See also Rule of St. Francis
lay communities, women's
   acquisition of religious identity by, 41–42, 43
   associated with religion, 35–37

attraction of, 41
characteristics of, 61
disappearance of, 49–50, 62
economic structure of, 61
flexibility of, 62
formation of, 41, 42
and Francis's ideal, 62
goals of, 65
growing control of, 49, 62, 64, 65, 71
and heresy, 42, 64
production of saints in, 43
religiosity of, 72
rules for, 37
suspicion of, 41, 62
transformation of, 62, 65
See also beguines
lay-pietism, 37
Legenda di Perugia, 7, 9, 12
Legenda of Santa Chiara, 67, 68–70
Legenda Perusina, 7, 9, 12
Leo, 7
Leo's scroll, 14
Letter of Greccio, 7
Licet Apostolica Sedes (Innocent III), 18
light, 67–68
Little, Lester K., 83
love, 13

Malatesta, Battista of Montefeltro, 62, 65–71
Manselli, Raoul, 7–8, 9, 26, 29
Margherita da Cortona, 3, 43–49
Martha, 91, 92
Mary, 91, 92
Mary Magadalena, 45
Mascari, Marinaria, 47
Mascari (family), 47
Masters, 91, 92, 95, 103, 108
Meersseman, G. G., 35–36, 37, 42, 75–76
Merlo, G. G., 29, 30, 32
ministry, 96
minores, 53, 73, 84, 87, 114
  See also paupertas; poverty
minoritas, 53, 73, 74, 78, 97, 114
  See also paupertas; poverty
Mira circa nos (Gregory IX), 24
mirror, 8
monasteries
  creation of, 64
  goals of, 65

See also see also convents; Santa Lucia,
  Monastery of
Monastery of Santa Lucia. *See* Santa Lucia,
  Monastery of
money
  Francis's attitude toward, 77, 80, 81, 90
  in Later Rule, 82
  in new economy, 83
  Olivi on, 102, 103
  possession of, 102
  use of, and poverty, 86
  and use of agents, 90–91, 103
  and work, 93

Nelli, René, 43
Newman, Barbara, 40
Nicholas III, 102, 104, 105
Nimis iniqua (Gregory IX), 87
*Nos qui cum eo fuimus, Contributo alla
  questione francescana* (Manselli), 7–8, 9
nuntius, 90–91, 103

obedience, 100, 109–10
Olivi, Peter of John
  on begging, 107
  Clareno's *Epilogus* for, 113
  commentary on Rule, 97–108
  as economist, 101–2
  failure to associate work with poverty, 114
  misuse of writings of, 75
  persecution of, 108
  referred to by Clareno, 109
  sincerity of, 107
  social agenda of, 100–101
  style of, 103
  as symbol for Spirituals, 108
Ordo Fraternitatis (Meersseman), 35–36
Orsini, Napoleone, 45
Osservanza, 60, 65
ownership, 92–93, 94–95

Paciocco, Roberto, 20–21
Padua, 21–22, 24, 25, 31, 40
Papal Infallibility, 19
Papi, Anna Benvenuti, 38, 46, 49
Paradiso (Dante), 67–68
Parenti, Giovanni, 22
St. Paul, 106, 107
Paul of Thebes, 113

paupertas
  concept of, 53, 73, 78
  in Hugh's commentary, 94–95
  in *Sacrum Commercium,* 56
  separated from labor/work, 85, 114
  See also poverty
peace, 55–56, 77
Pecham, John, 30, 97
Pelligrini, Luigi, 81
penance, 11, 45, 46, 47, 48
Pini, Antonio Ivan, 80
Pirandello, Luigi, 5, 8
Piron, Sylvain, 99
poems
  attributed to Hyeronima Battista, 67
  Legenda of Santa Chiara, 67, 68–70
  of Vigri, 71
politics, religion's connection with, 34
Polizzi, Carlo, 27
Pope
  sanctity of, 19
  See also individual popes
poverty
  Aquinas on, 97
  and begging, 87, 90, 93, 95–96, 103, 105, 107
  Bonaventure on, 97
  and commercial revolution, 53, 54
  commitment to, 73
  debate over, 97
  degrees of, 95
  and disappearance of work, 99
  and economy, 101–2
  in everyday practice, 97, 107
  failure of within religious communities, 56–57
  Francis's commitment to, 53, 114
  in Hugh's commentary, 92, 94–95
  importance of, 57, 83, 98
  included in vows, 99–100
  Lady Poverty, 52, 55, 56, 57, 73, 85
  maintenance of, 91
  Olivi on, 97–108
  Pecham on, 97
  and tension within brotherhood, 52
  and use of money, 86
  usus pauper controversy, 98–108
  views of, 53
  See also paupertas

poverty, evangelical, 103
power, 106, 107
prayer, 92, 105, 106, 112
preaching, 54, 87, 89, 105, 106
Proust, Marcel, 5
Provence, 101

Questions on Evangelical Perfection (Olivi), 98, 99, 100, 101
Quo elongati (Gregory IX), 21, 23, 52, 53, 54, 74, 86–87, 94
Quoniam abundavit (Gregory IX), 87

Reggimento e costumi di donna (Francesco da Barberino), 48–49
religion
  connection with politics and economy, 34
  lay communities associated with, 35–37
religiosity
  attitudes toward, 76
  and convents, 63–64
  in Francis's community, 75
  of lay communities, 72
  in medieval environment, 75–76
Rigaldina, 30
Right you are if you think so (Pirandello), 5
Rigon, Antonio, 30
Rimini, 30
Rizzardo of Sambonifacio, 25
Rolandino, 22
Rome, as center of Christianity, 45–47
Rufino, 7
The Rule, Profession, Life and True Calling of a Lesser Brother, 9
Rule of St. Francis
  and Anthony, 23
  changes to, 12, 85
  Clareno's commentary on, 109–13
  confusion regarding, 89
  as divine inspiration, 109, 110
  Hugh of Digne's commentary on, 88–97
  image of Francis in, 10, 12
  indivisibility of from *Testament,* 111
  interpretation of, 21, 23, 52 (*See also Quo elongati*)
  and obedience, 100, 109–10
  Olivi's commentary on, 97–109
  prohibition of glosses of, 10, 89

Quo elongati, 21, 23, 52, 53, 54, 74, 86–87, 94
  transformation of, 74, 90 (*See also Quo elongati*)
  translation of, 80, 93 (*See also "ars"*)
  See also Early Rule; Later Rule; *Testament*

Sabatier, Paul, 6, 8–9
Sacrum Commercium
  as allegory, 52–53
  author of, 54, 56
  date of, 51–52
  Francis's actions in, 52
  relationship to history, 52–53
  story in, 56
sainthood
  attitudes toward, 28
  control over, 18
  Francis's rejection of, 74
  importance of, 20
  Pope as candidate for, 19
  See also canonization
saints
  and heresy, 44
  images of, 45
  local, 31
  need for, 40
  and political power, 31–32
  production of in lay communities, 43
  See also canonization
Salimbene, 88
Santa Chiara, Monastery of, 61–62
Santa Lucia, Monastery of
  beguines in, 50
  chronicle of, 62–63, 65
  founding of, 59–60
  intellectual activity in, 71, 72
  as scriptorium, 60
  spiritual direction of, 60
Schlager, B., 45
scholarship, monastic, 65–72
Scripta Leo-Angelo-Rufino (Brook), 7
scriptorium, Santa Lucia as, 60
Sei personaggi in cerca di autore (Pirandello), 5
Sensi, Mario, 64
Six characters in search of an author (Pirandello), 5

Speculum Perfectionis, A Mirror of Perfection, 8–9
spirituality
  Anthony's, 31
  Clare as representation of, 45
  competition with corporality, 91–92
  and dualism, 13–14
  Francis's, 74, 75
spirituality, Franciscan, 45
Spirituals, 75, 97, 98, 100, 107, 108, 109, 110, 111
study, as work, 105, 106
Sulmona, 59, 61
Svevo, Italo, 5
Sylvester I, 56

Tamassia, Nino, 8
Testament, Francis's
  in Clareno's commentary, 111, 112
  indivisibility of from Rule, 111
  judged as non-binding, 79, 86
  prohibition of glosses in, 89
  transformation of, 53–54 (*See also Quo elongati*)
  work in, 111
  writing of, 111
  See also Rule of St. Francis
Thomas Aquinas, 97
Thompson, Augustine, 21, 34, 38, 39, 61
The Three Companions, 7
Todeschini, Giacomo, 101
The Treatise on usus pauper (Olivi), 98
Trinci, Paoluccio, 60
Trinci (family), 59

Ubertino da Casale, 6, 7
Ugolino da Ostia, 23
  See also Gregory IX; Hugolino
Ugolino da Segni, 37
  See also Gregory IX; Hugolino
Umbria Serafica (Agostino da Stroncone), 59
university, 89–90
Urban IV, 60
usus pauper controversy, 98–108, 110–11

Varano, Costanza Varano, 65, 66
Varano, Elisabetta Varano, 65, 66
Vatican I, 19
Vauchez, A., 18, 19, 28–29, 35, 42–43, 75

Veneto region, 26, 27
Verona, 25, 26
Vigri, Caterina Vigri, 71
Vita prima, 20, 23
vows, 99–100

will, 99
women
   attraction of lay communities to, 41
   control of, 60
   control of bodies of, 44
   discrimination against, 56, 72
   education of, 70–71
   effects of political struggles on, 61–62
   expected to follow religious rules, 37
   Francesco da Barberino on, 48–49
   Margherita da Cortona, 43–49
   options for, 63, 64
   as part of Franciscan Order, 56
   reasons for entering religious communities, 60
   restrictions on, 56
   and social stability, 41
   See also beguines; Clare; convents; lay communities, women's; monasteries; Santa Lucia, Monastery of
work
   absence of from Clareno's commentary, 110–11
   alienation from, 87
   arguments for, 105–6
   "*ars*", 80, 81, 84, 85, 90, 112
   Augustine on, 106
   Basil on, 112–13
   in Clareno's commentary, 109–13
   disappearance of, 54, 74, 87, 99, 102–3
   in Early Rule, 74, 82, 88
   in *forma vitae,* 79–88
   Francis's ideal of, 84
   in Hugh of Digne's commentary, 88–97
   as labor, 81, 85, 90, 112
   in Later Rule, 82, 88
   and market economy, 84–85
   in medieval Italy, 80–81
   ministry as, 96
   and money, 93
   necessity of, 106
   Olivi on, 103–4, 105
   and ownership, 92
   Paul on, 106
   and power, 106
   and prayer, 92, 106
   purpose of, 104, 112
   separated from *paupertas,* 114
   study as, 105, 106
   in *Testament,* 111
   without pay, attitudes toward, 84
work, manual, 81, 85, 104, 105, 112
work, spiritual, 104
   See also ministry; prayer

Zeno's conscience (Svevo), 5
Zinelli, F., 67